Praise for the first book in the series: *A Church Dismantled—*
A Kingdom Restored: Why Is God Taking Apart the Church?

An excellent book for church leaders and congregants who in-
tuitively understand that "returning to normal" is not a realistic
or compelling vision for the future. Kanagy writes from many years
of pastoral ministry, as a sociology professor, and from challenging
personal experiences. Having been diagnosed with Parkinson's disease
at a relatively young age, he models a depth of vulnerability not often
seen in pastors or professors. He writes with hope while being painfully honest about his personal struggles and the failures of the church
to fully represent the Jesus many claim to follow.
      - Loren Swartzendruber, University President Emeritus

The content of this book started as a podcast during the pandemic
that resonated quickly and reached hundreds of congregants and
souls during a time when most were asking when or if "normal" would
ever return. It is shared as a collection of essays in a story-telling style
that is easy to read and gives both every-day and Biblical context to
the search for meaning during such polarizing rapidly changing times.
Flavored from his experiences as a neighbor, a sociology professor, a
pastor, and as one who has been recently diagnosed with Parkinson's
disease—Conrad heralds a prophetic call of hope for the big C-Church,
and calls those who may feel despair at the level of the local everyday
church pew to rise up and ask the question "What are You up to God,
and how can I be part of Your grand plan?"
      - Anne Reed Love, Author

I don't throw around the term "prophetic," but it's actually the word
that I'd use to describe "A Church Dismantled." Kanagy calls us to
see honestly "what is" and look ahead hopefully to what is becoming
and might come to be. He vulnerably shares his own journey in a way
that invites me, as the reader, to think deeply about where my own
vulnerability can build relationships and connections with others in
a hurting world. This is a timely book and a breath of fresh air in the
midst of fear, division, and "othering."
      - Jon Heinly, Educator

Kanagy is a contemporary prophet who has written a bracing collection of personal vignettes and diagnostic oracles. They remind me especially of the Prophet Jeremiah—the weeping prophet of doom and of promise. The book is easy to read. It is vivid, unflinching in its honesty, and often brilliant in observation. God is dismantling the human structures and strategies of the western church. But this is no dirge; Kanagy is not a funeral director. From a place of deep anguish, he writes passionately with hope about God's deeper and bigger purposes. God is up to something, as always, though we fail to see it. The debris of the western church is no exception. No church dismantled, no kingdom restored. No cross, no resurrection or crown.

- Mark R. Wenger, Pastor

From letters to the congregation in the beginning of the CO-VID-19 pandemic to blogs to a book. In 38 chapters, Conrad Kanagy makes the reader think about what is happening to the institutionalized church. Having experienced a personal dismantling through the diagnosis of Parkinson's disease and having learned to listen anew to what the Spirit is telling, Kanagy urges the churches to use the forced closures during the pandemic to start listening to what God wants from us. Not going back to the "normal" situation from before but really explore how they can be church, people of God, followers of Jesus. This writer is inspired, the text describes sometimes moving personal experiences, sometimes more observations from a distance but always inspiring. Very worthwhile reading for everybody who is interested in being part of the living church in a changing world.

- Henk W. Stenvers, Dutch Mennonite Leader

MINISTRY
IN A CHURCH DISMANTLED

*To Tear Down
or Build Up?*

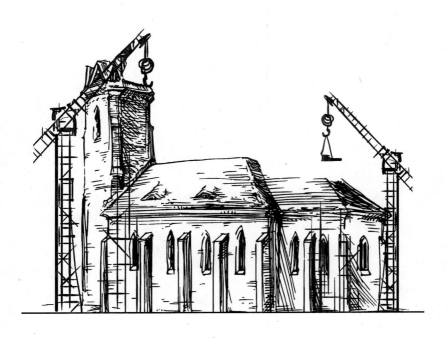

CONRAD L. KANAGY

MINISTRY IN A CHURCH DISMANTLED
To Tear Down or Build Up?
by Conrad L. Kanagy

Scripture quotations unless noted otherwise are from *The New Revised Standard Version of the Bible* (NRSV), copyright © 1989, Division of Christian Education of the National Council of the Churches of Christ in the United States of America. Used by permission. All rights reserved.

Selection from Henk Stenvers, "Walking on Water," Part 1, "Concerning the Future of the Dutch Mennonites" (Algemene Doopsgezinde Societëit), Feb. 3, 2021, reprinted with the author's permission.

Library of Congress Control Number: 2021947678
International Standard Book Number: 978-1-60126-761-0

Masthof Press
219 Mill Road | Morgantown, PA 19543-9516
www.Masthof.com

MORE BY
CONRAD L. KANAGY

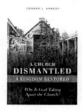

*A Church Dismantled—A
Kingdom Restored: Why Is
God Taking Apart the
Church?* Morgantown,
PA: Masthof Press, 2021.

*Winds of the Spirit: A Profile of Anabap-
tist Churches in the Global South.* (with
Richard Showalter and Tilahun Beyene),
Harrisonburg, VA: Herald Press, 2012.

*Road Signs for the Journey:
A Profile for Mennonite
Church USA.* Harrison-
burg, VA: Herald Press,
2007.

The Riddles of Human Society (with
Donald Kraybill), California: Pine Forge
Press, 1999.

TO JACOB AND SARAH

You have listened often to my "ministry stories"
and sermon "highlight reels," always offering
insightful feedback, support and encouragement—
how grateful to God I am for you both!

"All will be whole and powerful again . . .
A race of loyal herders and tall plowmen."

—*Reynolds Price, "All Will Be Whole" (after Rilke)*

TABLE OF CONTENTS

FOREWORD

In this second book in the series—"A Church Dismantled"—Conrad Kanagy looks objectively at our society and church communities, both as a sociologist of religion as well as a Mennonite pastor who is faithfully leading a vibrant congregation while experiencing the challenges and heartaches of authentic ministry. Conrad's ability to blend those two vocations is evident in this book.

A sociologist is often considered prophetic because they see what others overlook and even deny. A pastor often experiences his or her congregation and community at a level of reality that is not apparent to others in the church. Conrad melds both of these realities together and somehow discovers a real element of hope that "just may lead us" through the entanglements and challenges that 2020 and beyond have created for the Church. Conrad points to a hope that is found in a kingdom birthed by Christ and restored through the work of the Holy Spirit.

He documents pastors and church leaders who are now confronted by realities that refuse to allow them and their congregations to simply "return to normal" or to re-engage what was "before." These realities demand that Christ followers are led by the Spirit into the kingdom that Jesus spoke of so often and longed for us to experience. Leaders are struggling to address multiple challenges and pastors are attempting to shepherd divided congregants, even while addressing the varied needs of their communities. As I meet with pastors, they consistently express the desire that they not be guilty of leading simply an enterprise, but truly a movement of God.

Conrad offers insights as a pastor and a sociologist into how we might see a church forever changed and embrace a kingdom restored, a kingdom that is an answer to the prayer of Jesus that the Father's "will be done on earth as it is in heaven" (Matthew 6:10). Unsettling at times, this book is filled with hope as we face these new realities.

–Rev. Eldon Fry, D.Min.
Founder of Open Hands Ministries

INTRODUCTION

This book, written over the past year, is the second in the four-book series entitled "A Church Dismantled—A Kingdom Restored," based upon the popular podcast by the same name that I produced during the Covid-19 pandemic in 2020-21. That podcast included many episodes relevant to spiritual leaders, ministers, and pastors, and the unique challenges they faced during the pandemic and continue to face. While the first book, *A Church Dismantled—A Kingdom Restored: Why Is God Taking Apart the Church?* is a kind of sampler of the podcast episodes while also serving as a foundation that lays out the major themes of the series, this book and the remaining ones in the series will each address specific themes found in that first volume but upon which I expand in each respective new release.[1]

When I began to write the podcast episodes in May, 2020, I had no intention of stepping down from local congregational ministry any time soon. My wife, Heidi and I had been serving the same congregation for nearly fifteen years and enjoyed our ministry together. But as the months dragged by, and the combined impact of ministry stress and the emotional thinness of my life due to the continued progression of Parkinson's disease, we made a decision that I would retire by the end of 2021. In some ways perhaps, this book documents the evolution in my own ministry journey and changing sense of call across the lengthy season of the pandemic and political polarization experienced by an already weakened and fragile American church, whose dis-

---

[1]   Conrad L. Kanagy, *A Church Dismantled—A Kingdom Restored: Why Is God Taking Apart the Church?* (Morgantown: Masthof Press, 2021).

mantling only seems to have accelerated in the past eighteen months. The current book is organized according to various ministry related themes. To provide a contextual timeframe, each chapter indicates the month in which it was written.

The subtitle of the book—To Tear Down or Build Up?—reflects the dilemma that we pastors find ourselves in during the current context of the American church. Book upon book offers guidance as to how to rebuild your church, change your church, transform your church, and on and on. Indeed, just like for the individual an entire industry of self-help materials have emerged offering to remake, restore, transform and more, so such an industry of church experts has arisen with promises of salvation in tow.

This book offers no such promise and points to the fact that the biblical record so often includes destruction, "plucking down," and lowering mountains as part of what God is up to in the Church and the world, and in your life and my life. I have received plenty of resistance to this message, perhaps because for some it seems so "unGod-like." But if I cannot believe that the desolation I see all around me does not include the providential hand of God, then frankly, I am left without hope. And so are you. But if I can claim and even glimpse the Almighty's shadow in the midst of everything crumbling around me, than once again hope returns!

For me, dismantling the Church is about joining God's grand excavation project of Isaiah 40 (which has captured my imagination ever since I was a child), by lowering mountains that are barriers to the shalom of God's coming kingdom, by raising valleys in which the marginalized have had to hide for fear of being overrun by those who hold the power strings, by making crooked paths straight and rough places a level plain along which the lost, the wounded, and the destitute may find their way home. Contrary to the vision of Isaiah, the Church too often has done the opposite, by erecting mountains, deepening valleys, and making pathways rougher and more crooked than they already were.

Which brings me to the second aspect of what I mean by the Spirit's dismantling of the Church. That is the removal of those "mantles" of our own devising that we have placed on the Church and the Christian faith. These cover up the truths of God's kingdom that we are called to live by as our truths.

The dismantling that I identify in this book has been both personal and autobiographical, as I confess my own false mantles while also calling out the false mantles of the Church that have displaced the true mantle of Christ—whether those false mantles be imposed upon any one or all of us, or upon God, or upon the Church itself.

From very early on as a child, I was caught in cycles of torment and depression characteristic of obsessive-compulsiveness, which were fed by the oppressiveness of an "old order" of cultural fog that emphasized goodness, performance, perfection, and, on top of it all, God's wrath. So whenever I failed to hit the high mark, which was every moment of every day, I remember having these kinds of thoughts: *Am I the only sinner among this bunch of saints? Are all the others okay with their sins? Do they know some secret about how to survive with a guilty conscience, which no one has shared with me? I don't understand why everyone says the gospel is so wonderful, when to me, when often it feels like hell instead of good news.*

Slowly and over time, I began to understand that what the Church had done (and all too often still does) was to "mantle" (as in "muzzle") the truth, by declaring one thing while being altogether comfortable with something else. It would market its product with false advertising, claiming that the naked emperor wore a fine suit of clothes and that his wife wore a starched bonnet, but what I saw underneath was something altogether different.

To "mantle" means to cover up and smooth over. And, dear

folks, you and I both know that the Church has too often covered up truths and smoothed over falsehoods. It was recognizing the false mantles of the church for what they are that saved me from giving up on God. And I suspect that I will spend the rest of my days doing the work of dismantling if it means that even one more person could be set free, as I have been set free over the course of this past year—set free by the One named Jesus who so dismantled the religious arrogance and edifices of his day that it cost him his life in order to save the world.

In 2017, I was diagnosed with Parkinson's disease at the age of fifty-two. For the first year I cried and raged as I grieved the losses to come. But over time, I have also begun to recognize the gifts that I am receiving as a result of this disease. One of those gifts is the clarity with which I now see the horizon ahead, and the knowledge that my days of quality health are limited. This recognition has been transformative for me, as I realize that my own body is being dismantled at the same time that the Church itself is being dismantled. My weaknesses are being exposed; the mantles I wore to cover those weaknesses have been stripped away. I can't hide my vulnerabilities or deny my fragility. Over the past four years I have had a new conversion to Jesus and a new awareness of God's incredible love for his children—meaning every human being created with the imprint of God upon them. I have little doubt that the podcast or this book series would ever have emerged without this disease that took me by such surprise, but which I now realize is my own unique path home.

It has been clear to me during the past year that I am not alone in my sense that the Church is in the process of being dismantled. The podcast "A Church Dismantled—A Kingdom Restored" has appealed to many more listeners than I ever imagined it would. Nearly 50,000 episodes have been downloaded in more than eighty countries and nearly 1,600 cities. It seems my writing has had a special appeal to folks who have become disillusioned with the American Church and have perhaps left it. I call these folks "the diaspora"—those who have left what we have long presumed to be the primary institution by which one discovers the kingdom of God but which too often is the one that leads folks in the wrong direction or in no direction at all.

I have so many persons to acknowledge and thank for their support of this project over the past year and longer. I have walked with my wife Heidi for more than three decades, and she more than anyone has influenced my love for God's Word and the truths found in the holy scripture. I have been deeply formed by her and by our journey together and the ministry we have shared. Our collaboration has been one of the richest and most meaningful experiences of our life together. As I have pulled back in ministry due to my health, Heidi has expanded her own ministry while at the same time covering for me in those areas where I have had to make adjustments. She has become my strongest and most loyal advocate whose wisdom, courage, and capacity I increasingly rely upon. This new dependency upon Heidi reflects what I foresaw during our sabbatical in 2017, just after learning of my Parkinson's diagnosis—that I would still get home, but would do so by leaning on the shoulder of a friend.

Elizabethtown College for nearly three decades has given me space to engage in my church related research and practice of ministry. Across four college administrations I have been blessed by the same support and encouragement, without which I would not have been able to "pastor" as a minister and "profess" as a teacher at the same time. In keeping with what I have always experienced, the college has supported and promoted the podcast "A Church Dismantled—A Kingdom Restored" and has publicized my efforts widely. The college has also given me a sabbatical for the fall of 2021 to continue to write and publish my work.

The pastors and spiritual leaders who have shaped me over the years, particularly in light of my own lack of seminary training: My grandfather Erie "Pap" Renno, Gerald Peachey, Guy Rocker, Max Zook, E. Daniel Martin, Richard Frank, Keith Weaver, Keith Yoder, Eldon Fry, Stan Shantz and many others.

Our congregation at Elizabethtown Mennonite Church has graciously been a space for me over the last decade to hone my preaching and writing for an audience that lives and labors in the everyday world of work, home, and play.

Trinity McFadden copyedited the manuscript and Linda Boll proofread with a keen eye for discovering errors others of us had missed—I am particularly grateful for her assistance. I wish to thank my cover designers Mark Aquino and Elizabeth Petersheim (Masthof Press) for their creative and attractive work.

Dan Mast and the staff of Masthof Press have been a valued collaborator on this project, speeding the project along, marketing the book, and being extremely organized, nimble and responsive in every way. Frankly, I cannot imagine a better publishing partner!

I also want to thank my podcast listeners of the past year and the members of my Facebook group "A Church Dismantled" for their ambitious collaboration and their ongoing support. They have been a consistent source of affirmation and have helped me to feel less homeless and less alone in this dismantled church.

Thanks go to publicist Rob Eagar for his excellent counsel and direction in thinking about how to market this book and those that follow.

Finally, I am grateful for the willingness of my long-time spiritual director, Eldon Fry to write the Foreword for the book. Eldon has taught me much, including that "God does not shame me" and that "God is not the church," both of which I have recalled time and again in the midst of doubt, fear, shame and resistance as a local congregational pastor. Eldon's wisdom is timeless and his support has enabled me to minister as long as I have done so.

Nearly all of these essays were written during the Covid pandemic. I have sought to retain, for the most part, the present tense in which they were originally penned. This book and the podcast episodes that preceded it represent for me the intersection and integration of various areas of my professional and personal life that had been disparate entities in the past. They have allowed me to draw upon nearly three decades of teaching sociology, thirty-five years of sociological research, fifteen years of church and denominational consulting, twenty years of pastoral ministry, my childhood and coming-of-age in a conservative Mennonite-Amish community, my life-long struggle with a terror of God's wrath exacerbated by obsessive-compulsive disorder, and the diagnosis, four years ago, of Parkinson's disease.

My prayer is that my reflections throughout this book, and the previous as well as future volumes, *In a Church Dismantled—The Light Still Shines: Reflections in Sacred Time* and *A Dismantled Church and One Pilgrim's Journey: Finding My Way Home in the Dark* will be an encouragement to you, and will cast a bit of light on your own journey toward the new heaven and new earth that is just over the horizon.

So, accompanied by the gracious words of the apostle Paul, himself plagued by weakness and troubled with a thorn in the flesh that God would not remove, may you receive my words, like Paul's, as means of encouragement. For, in the midst of the dismantling: "We do not lose heart. Even though our outer nature is wasting away, our inner nature is being renewed day by day. For this slight momentary affliction is preparing us for an eternal weight of glory beyond all measure, because we look not at what can be seen but at what cannot be seen; for what can be seen is temporary, but what cannot be seen is eternal" (2 Cor 4:16–18).

–Conrad L. Kanagy, Elizabethtown, PA
September 3, 2021

READERS' RESOURCES:

The website www.achurchdismantled.com contains resources to support the material in this book, including a short video in which I address each of the eight sections of the book as well as study guides for personal or group reflection and discussion. Readers may contact me directly through the website as well as subscribe for continued updates about the book series and future projects.

PART ONE

PASTORS IN
AN IRON CAGE

CHAPTER 1

My Pastoral Word at the Outset of a Pandemic
May 2020

I n May of 2020, during the early months of the Covid pandemic, I wrote what I simply call the "Weekly Email" to our congregation, where my wife, Heidi, and I have served as a ministry couple for fifteen years. I titled that week's email message "Why the Church Cannot Be Reopened," which was my reaction to the incessant calls of local church leaders to "get back to church" as soon as possible.

That little piece caught the attention of a few folks, who then passed it on to others, which led to a series of blog-like postings on Facebook and eventually to a year-long podcast of 275 episodes. The primary theme of the podcast was at least fifteen years in the making and was based upon research on the American church that I conducted in 2006-2007, resulting in a book titled *Road Signs for the Journey*.[2]

At that time, I raised the question: "Is God's Spirit dismantling the church because we have so failed God's mission?" For me the question has now become rhetorical, since I do embrace the idea that God is up to a grand deconstruction or dismantling—a taking apart—of the Church as we know it and as it has been constructed in the West. This question was quickly followed by another: "If this is what God's Spirit is doing, then how can we as leaders work with the Spirit rather than against the Spirit?"

---

[2]   Conrad L. Kanagy, *Road Signs for the Journey* (Scottdale, PA: Herald Press, 2007).

At the onset of the Covid pandemic, I quickly saw this moment as a season rich with transformational opportunities for the Church, if only we would see and embrace them. Over the past century, the Church in the West has staked its future on the rational structures of modernity—on Enlightenment ideals about what is real and true and right and good. But little have we understood just how vulnerable we have made ourselves by doing so. It's almost as if some days we have thrown Jesus in as an afterthought. Over the years, I have repeatedly cautioned my students that we have no idea whether modernity is sustainable or not. When we embrace the cultures and structures of modernity, we are vulnerable to whatever attacks them.[3]

Given our confidence in the reliability of empiricism and science, the last thing we expected was an unpredictable and unknown virus to threaten the modern foundations upon which we have built the Church. My concern at the onset of the Covid pandemic was that if we failed to be honest about how thoroughly accommodated the Church had become to modernity, including its economic and political manifestations, then we were unlikely to weather the pain and discomfort of the Spirit's reorientation of the Church during the pandemic. I repeatedly stated, "If we are not converted to the ways of Jesus in this moment, we may never be."

And so I crafted a letter to our congregation to try to provide a holy context for gaining traction in our life with God while in the midst of the pandemic:

> Greetings in Christ's precious name. After a week of sharing prophetic reflections on Facebook about where we are and the meaning of what I sense God is up to, I want to share with

---

[3]   In recognizing the reality that the local church is part of the universal Church, even if it so often fails to reflect the qualities of Christ's bride, I use the upper and lower case "C" interchangeably.

you a more pastoral message on how I sense God is resetting us.

In doing so I want to plead with you to stay grounded in God. No matter what President Trump says or Governor Wolf says or CNN or MSNBC say or FOX News or Rush Limbaugh say, please first of all ask the Lord what he is saying—spend more time with the Lord than listening to any of these other voices. The problem for God's people just before exile is that they failed to ask, "Where is the Lord?" Even the priests failed to ask, "Where is the Lord?" Friends, whatever happens and wherever we end up in all of this, please let us not be guilty of not having asked, "Lord, where are you?"

The next several weeks are critical ones for our congregation. Many congregations will be "reopening," and many voices will be emerging and swirling around us, and some of you may feel that pressure to respond to questions of, "When is your congregation reopening?" I want to encourage you to lovingly respond that, "The church has been open all along," and that we will, "Reassemble once we have collectively heard from the Lord what he is saying about how we reset going forward into his future." This approach is not about ultimately resisting the government nor taking our orders directly from the government—it is about listening to the King of kings and the One who is writing the story that is taking us to the new heaven and new earth. It is about doing what the Church is always to do—listening to its Leader and the One who is our Maker and Creator.

When we only focus on, "When do we reopen?" and, "How do we reopen?", we are only focusing on mere technicalities, such as where to put the hand sanitizer and whether to wear masks or not and how to socially distance, etc. These are merely technical changes that do nothing to address the deep spiritual and cultural changes that God is up to at this time.

Even questions about whether resetting involves continuing to livestream our services, using electronic bulletins, using Zoom for certain meetings, etc., are still at the technical level rather than the deeper adaptive level of change that addresses our corporate sins and habits and ways of doing things that have gotten in the way of the Spirit having its way in us.

My concern is how we have accepted and absorbed a world that made us tired, that kept us fragmented and disordered, that placed ourselves at the center and put Jesus on the outside, that abandoned the poor and marginalized—white, black, brown, citizen, undocumented non-citizen, widow, Republican, Democrat, divorcee, addict, felon, gay and straight, young and old, the one who just had an abortion and the one who gave away her child for adoption, Christian and not. Our political allegiances, our self-centeredness, our ways of always doing things have all gotten in the way of sharing Christ's love with them—these who, like you and me, are created in God's image and have his imprint upon them. We will be and likely are being judged for these sins, just as God's people were in the sixth century B.C.

I plead with you to abandon political allegiances—right and left—that have kept you from truly asking, "Where is the Lord?" For a moment, please hear me. I am not saying that it is a sin to vote or to be involved in the political process, but I am pleading with you to spend as much time with God as you do getting input from your favorite news outlet and that you not filter God's Word through what you hear these outlets saying but that you filter what they are saying through what you heard God saying to you this morning.

If we do not reset our engagement in the political process as a Church, we will find ourselves in a day when it will be safer to be a true follower of Jesus in the world than in the Church, and maybe that is what needs to happen to get us out of the Church and into the world with the message that God so loved the world and loves it still.

Nearly all of Jesus's last words to his disciples included the mandate that they were being sent not into the Church but into the world. And they were going out like sheep among wolves. He never promises safety, but he assures them that he will never leave them nor forsake them. And he promises them authority. And he promises them joy. And all of this he can promise because in a few days he will be sending the Spirit.

You see, the forty days of resetting between Jesus's death and resurrection included resetting the disciples to receive the Spirit and to prepare them to be reset by that same Spirit. Reset for what? The answer occurs immediately after the tongues of fire and the mighty wind: reset for God's mission, reset to tell the good news to Jerusalem, Judea, Samaria, and the ends of the earth.

But this reset involved ceasing from their daily activities and quarantining in a room together until the Spirit of God came to them. My concern with the rush to get back to church—and, frankly, to get back to anything that created bondage for us and kept us away from our First Love, including church—is that we will not pause long enough in this transition to receive the resetting of the Spirit anew, a resetting that will result in a revelation of our deepest sins and confession of these, a resetting that will move us more fully into God's mission to the world.

Who of us will be reset by the Spirit? Who of us will repent of lives that took us further from God than closer to him? I am confident that despite Christ's offer of life, some of us, even given that chance after death, will still choose hell over heaven because we have done so all of our lives. This Covid crisis has come in part to give us the chance to once again choose heaven. Inevitably, some will remain in their hell. But damnation is not our destiny, folks—the new heaven and new earth are!

But as the months rolled along, I began to sense frustration among some of the saints, who wondered, "Conrad, just what do you mean by the dismantling of the Church, and how long will you keep rattling the same cage?"

I responded that I believe the Spirit is deconstructing, or tear-ing down, or taking apart the socially constructed elements of the Church that recently have become—or for a long time have been— irrelevant to the central message of the gospel. That is to say, ways of being the Church that have lost sight of the essential meaning and purpose of the Church, ways of interpreting scripture that have justified remaining culture-bound and period-bound, and ways of forming political alliances with principalities and powers, which has terribly compromised the message of Jesus.

This deconstruction may require eliminating tiresome com- mittee meetings, which often spend more time discussing who will clean the church than on who will care for the diversity of neigh- bors in all degrees of circumstances surrounding the church. These meetings will spend time on anything that can take our eyes off the imperatives of the gospel, to which Jesus urgently summons us in mission. Parenthetically, our youth flee the Church, not as pagans who renounce the Church, but as insightful persons who see more clearly than the rest of us just what the Church has become.

When I left ministry the first time, I discovered the existence of missional theology, which was so very helpful in understanding the condition of the Church and what was required for its transfor- mation and renewed faithfulness. But fifteen years later and after a decade of working intentionally at a radically different model of ministry and mission, I am now uncertain whether the Church in the West is willing to take the steps to operationalize this theology and to be obedient to God's missional calling.

I have come to believe now that what we need is less a theology of mission and more a theology of "dismantling" that is consistent with the story of a God throughout history who intervenes to undo and tear down when God's people are stuck in the wildernesses of our own doing. This book series is in some ways an effort at develop- ing such a theology, and the fact that it has resonated with so many other folks suggests to me that more of us are ready for the same divine answer.

CHAPTER 2

The Iron Cage of Modernity and the Recovery of a Model Wherein Every Member Ministers

October 2019 (Pre-covid)

When Heidi and I were called back in 2011 to lead Elizabethtown Mennonite Church for the second time, having ministered in that congregation from 2000-2005, we came with a set of priorities that included deconstructing the exclusiveness of the professional ministry model, minimizing the distance between clergy and laity, seeing every member as a minister, and removing the barriers between the church and the community around it. We did so intentionally, recognizing this as a missional experiment.

But this was not always my approach to ministry. When I was called to ministry in 2000, I read John Piper's book *Brothers, We Are Not Professionals*. I reacted negatively to that book, fiercely opposed to the idea that pastoral ministry was not professional. But by 2007, when I was deep into my study of the American Church, and someone asked me, "What is the greatest crisis facing the Church?" my immediate response was "the professionalization of the clergy."

In saying that, I want to note that my critique is not of any of us in particular, nor does it invalidate the incredible leadership of so many pastors and ministers, the suffering they have experienced in ministry, the frustration they have felt, nor the contributions they have made. My critique is with a structure that has tended to shut down the calling of leaders and to create the perception of exclusivity, even when that is not the intention of any of us.

Results from my research in 2006-07 of American church members and leaders, showed that when asked about their expectations for their ministry role, pastors responded that they wanted to preach, cast vision, and equip the members for ministry. When members were asked what they expected of their pastors, they responded that they wanted pastors to preach and to take care of them. The difference between these two sets of expectations is a major reason so many congregations are in conflict, why so many pastors burn out, why pastors are difficult to find, why members fail to engage in ministry opportunities in their congregations, and why congregations do not achieve the mission God has called them to carry out. When pastors become paid and contracted professionals, we are suddenly subject to several hundred "employers" (depending on size of congregation of course) and are expected to carry the primary responsibility for the "success" of the congregation's mission. Those same pastors also join an elite and exclusive club of ministry professionals with degrees, credentials, and income.

When this occurs, members can disengage from ministry, and in doing so are free to criticize the pastor rather than to see themselves as empowered by the Holy Spirit to be part of the ministry and mission of the Church. A division between those ministering and those being ministered to occurs that is not healthy or biblical or consistent with the Reformation model of an "all believers' priesthood." And when the pastor leaves, congregations often struggle because the professional ministry model is too often individual-centric rather than ministry/mission-centric. The church goes out and hires a new pastor who brings in a new vision and changes things up and starts all over again. To be effective, the mission requires that we raise up some level of leadership from within our congregations.

I concluded from my research at the time that healthy and growing congregations and those fulfilling their missional call rec-

ognize that every member is a minister or a missionary with a calling and with spiritual gifts. In these congregations, the gap between
clergy and laity is minimized and the elite clergy class disappears as
the mission of God comes into view.

When I think of the Church these days, I go back to Max Weber,
a sociologist in the early 1900s who predicted that modernity would
result in an iron cage of rationality. He said that in embracing the rationality of the Enlightenment, humanity would abandon mystery and
imagination and lock itself into bureaucratic processes that appeared efficient and rational on the surface, but which would become inefficient
and irrational in reality. As a pastor now exiting my own congregation,
I am painfully aware of how the church and its structures, organization,
and formally rational ways have gutted a sense of the incredible mystery
of Christ and the Gospel, and how desperately such a recovery is needed
not only in my own life but in the Protestant church in this country.

Weber said this: "No one knows who will live in this cage in
the future, or whether at the end of this tremendous development
entirely new prophets will arise, or there will be a great rebirth of old
ideals, or, if neither, mechanized petrification embellished with a sort
of convulsive self-importance. For of the last stage of this cultural
development it might well be truly said: "Specialists without spirit,
sensualists without hear..."[4]

---

[4]   In his book *The McDonaldization of Society* (California: Pine Forge Press, 1993),
social theorist George Ritzer addresses the qualities of "modernity" or what we mean
when we describe the modern world. Throughout the book you will hear me describe
the "formal rationality" of the modern world, by which we mean that the world is organized in efficient and bureaucratic ways and through social institutions such as government, the economy, education, religion, health care, and more. These institutions are
organized in ways that have come to "make sense" to us and that are largely structured
according to formal rules, procedures, and regulations or what we often call "red tape."
Formal rationality has come to dominate modernity as predicted a century ago by German sociologist Max Weber, who argued that the bureaucracies resulting from such rationality would lead to all of us being captured within an "iron cage of rationality." Max
Weber, *Economy and Society* (Cambridge: Harvard University Press, 2019 [1922]).

Adapting Weber's notion of the iron cage to the ways in which the Church is stuck, we might paraphrase Weber this way: "No one knows who will minister in this cage in the future, or whether at the end of this tremendous development entirely new missional prophets will arise, or if there will be a great rebirth of old missional ideals, or, if neither, the result will be missional and ministry petrification embellished with a sort of convulsive and professional self-importance . . ."

What is my beef with the professionalization of the clergy? First, it is not the "priesthood of believers" recovered in the Protestant Reformation. Second, it is very recent (within the last two or three generations) for my Anabaptist tradition and has led to our difficulties in developing and calling new leaders. Third, it has prevented us from developing an every-member-a-minister culture and led to only-a-professionally-trained-pastor culture. I hear us talk far too often that if we can just get a pastor, then everything in our congregation will be okay again. But just getting a pastor is not ever going to solve our missional calling—too often it is a technical fix for what is a deeply spiritual and cultural problem.

What do I consider professional? Well, it is anything about ministry that creates a sense that we leaders are an exclusive group of people or in any way an elite class because of our credentials, education, status, language, or anything except God's calling on our lives and his Spirit empowering us. In the summer of 2019 I stumbled upon the writings of Rolland Allen, and I did a double take as I read his work from nearly one hundred years ago; I saw much of what I had been thinking for the last decade. Born in England in 1867, and a former missionary within the Anglican church, Allen was very opposed to the idea of mission stations that included all of the attachments of Western culture and education that missionaries brought with them. He believed in what he called the "spontaneous expansion of the Church" in which local, indigenous churches were

the key to the growth and spread of the gospel. He closely studied
the apostle Paul's methods and saw in Paul a great simplicity to the
spread of the gospel that he desperately appealed to the Anglican
church to replicate. Said Allen:

> This then is what I mean by spontaneous expansion. I
> mean the expansion which follows the unexhorted and unorga-
> nized activity of individual members of the Church explaining
> to others the Gospel which they have found for themselves; I
> mean the expansion which follows the irresistible attraction of
> the Christian Church for men who see its ordered life, and are
> drawn to it by desire to discover the secret of a life which they
> instinctively desire to share. . . .[5]

Allen promoted the idea of local, indigenous churches that
"managed their own local affairs under the leadership of their own
officers . . . administered their own sacraments . . . controlled their
own finance, and they propagate themselves, establishing in neighboring towns or villages Churches like themselves."[6]

For Allen, "indigenous" meant self-governing, self-supporting,
and self-extending. It did not rely on a larger organization for support, and he saw no distinction between church plants and fully established churches; they were all churches of Christ. Allen believed
that only local, indigenous churches could propagate themselves,
and a metric of whether a church was truly indigenous was whether
it was in fact "propagating itself on the soil."[7]

---

[5]   Roland Allen, *The Spontaneous Expansion of the Church: And the Causes Which Hinder It*. American ed. (Grand Rapids, MI: Wm. B. Eerdmans, 1962), 7.
[6]   Roland Allen, "The Essentials of an Indigenous Church," *World Dominion* 3 (1925), 111.
[7]   Roland Allen, "The Use of the Term Indigenous," *The International Review of Mission* 16 (1927), 262.

For Roland Allen, his opposition to the stipendiary system of the Anglican church represented that exclusivity. Said Allen:

> That Churches do not spring up where they live is due to the modern tradition that no church can be established anywhere without a particular type of cleric especially trained and set apart and paid. It is due to the fact that all our Christians are today taught this tradition and are so bound by it that their hands are tied and their spiritual power is atrophied. This tradition is so powerful that the establishment of new Churches by the scattering of Christians seems today almost a revolutionary doctrine.[8]

Allen resented the efforts of missionary societies to control the spontaneous expansion of the Church. In his view, only a church free of control could propagate. He argued that Paul practiced a process of devolution, meaning that Paul recognized the spiritual authority of the local, indigenous church at the time of its origins. There was no moment of handing the church off once its leaders were mature or the church had a sufficient number of members. While Allen had fears about the loss of central control of these new churches, he also argued that losing that control was consistent with Paul's church planting methods and made sense since the Holy Spirit was clearly at work in these new churches. This allowed Paul to speak glowingly of the churches in the epistles despite their on-the-ground reality— because he recognized them as peers with him in the gospel project rather than as novices to be paternalized.

In 2008-2010 I completed a survey of Anabaptist churches in the Global South. What amazed me was the fact that these congregations have no trouble identifying new leaders and that profes-

---

[8]   Roland Allen, "Voluntary Service in the Mission Field," *World Dominion* 5 (1927), 136.

sionalism (to the extent that it exists) is secondary to the call that one has from God to minister. I discovered a quote by a sociologist who studied other Global Southern churches, which impacted me greatly:

> [T]he genius of Pentecostalism is that it was a populist religion which affirmed the "priesthood of all believers," and so the missionaries could easily be replaced by indigenous leaders . . . anyone who was called by the Holy Spirit could be a minister of the gospel, which resulted in many bi-vocational clergy—even to this day. These men and women were powered by the Spirit rather than by titles, salaries, and pension plans. Many Pentecostal clergy have little formal theological training. Instead, they are schooled in the biblical narratives of personal transformation and find empirical verification for their beliefs in self-transcending experiences *where God intervenes in their life.*[9]

This quote so captures what I believe about the church and about leadership in the Church—empowered by the Holy Spirit and God's call rather than titles, credentials, and income. Interestingly, this model that Miller identifies is actually a very old model and one that we may well need to recover in dismantled Church, where we may need to rely on bi-vocational leaders called from within their congregations.

Credentialing was a largely mainline Protestant response to the rationalization of the twentieth century. They awarded a credential to those who had gone through college and seminary and now had earned the right to step into the pulpit. It was an accommodation to the rationality of the modern world in which all fields sought to offer credentials to those who were trained specialists.

---

[9]   Donald E. Miller, "Progressive Pentecostalism: An Emergent Trend in Global Christianity," *Journal of Beliefs and Values* 30 (2009), 284.

But what about the stay-at-home mom with a calling on her life to minister? What about Joe the Plumber who knows his calling is to ministry? What about the teenager who will be lucky just to finish high school but stays up nights rehearsing sermons that God has laid on his heart? What about the lifelong farmer whose evangelistic gift no one has ever called? What about the young couple whose family went through a spiritual revival that sent them to Bible college, but both are fully employed? What about folks who are sitting in our pews believing that because they lack the training and the credentials they have nothing to offer the mission of God?

What if they are filled with the Spirit, called by God to minister, and clearly reflect the gifts of the Spirit? Then what? What about them? The local church needs the capacity to nurture, call, and commission ministers without the cumbersome process of credentialing (a process that elevates some above others). If the local congregation is going to multiply, it will do so only as it is given the freedom to do the discerning and the calling and the commissioning without restrictions.

In other words, every member a missionary all of the time and everywhere, but especially in the local and indigenous context of the community within which the Church exists as the presence of Christ.

CHAPTER 3

What Weber Missed About the Iron Cage—the Spirit
May 2021

"A new heart I will give you, and a new spirit I will put within you; and I will remove from your body the heart of stone and give you a heart of flesh. I will put my spirit within you, and make you follow my statutes and be careful to observe my ordinances. Then you shall live in the land that I gave to your ancestors; and you shall be my people, and I will be your God." (Ezek. 36:26–28)

Last summer as I began this podcasting journey, I spent a lot of time discussing what Max Weber, a German sociologist at the turn of the twentieth century, described as the iron cage of the modern world. Weber believed, now more than one hundred years ago, that as we moderns continued our development, we would end up creating bureaucracies that would restrict our ability to create, imagine, and, in sum, become the human beings that God created us to be. Weber described this process as that of embracing "formal rationality," where social institutions increasingly rely upon policies and procedures and rules and regulations to guide them.

And Weber was exactly right. Look at just about any social institution these days and you will see paralysis—in government, health care, education, and, yes, the Church. And perhaps especially in the Church, in part because we were never meant to become a bureaucratic institution that mimicked modernity, but rather exist as a people of God. Weber argued that the only way out of the current dilemma would be the rise of charismatic leaders who would break through the iron cage and speak the truth—in other words, the prophets—and the recovery of ancient ideals or ideas. No other institution has a greater historic reservoir of both charisma and ancient ideals than the Church—if only we could recover them.

I have also argued in my book *Winds of the Spirit* that part of what has freed the global Southern Church and allowed for its greater vitality is indeed the fact that the Enlightenment, which led to formal rationality, had a lesser impact than in the West where the Enlightenment emerged.[10] But I have also cautioned that the impacts of globalization mean that the rationality of global Western modernity is infiltrating the Southern hemisphere and that there is no guarantee that the vitality we see today will continue tomorrow—that the iron cage just might find its way south as well and paralyze the work of God's Spirit that is so evident today.

Which brings us to the prophetic word of Dutch Mennonite leader Henk Stenvers, essay "Walking on Water."[11] For what Stenvers reveals is a Dutch Church, which, because of its decline, has broken the power of formal rationality and church bureaucracy, leaving only the people of God in its wake. Stenvers notes the increasing irrelevance of churchly councils, both locally at the congregational level and nationally at the denominational level. There are no longer enough members to attend the meetings or to fill the required positions.

In addition, as I have been arguing for fifteen years, the professional clergy model is disappearing. Congregations cannot afford to pay professional pastors, and so they are increasingly turning to lay

---

[10]   Conrad L. Kanagy, Richard Showalter, and Tilahun Beyene, *Winds of the Spirit* (Harrisonburg, VA: Herald Press, 2012).

[11]   Hank Stenvers, "Walking on Water," Part 1, "Concerning the Future of the Dutch Mennonites" (Algemene Doopsgezinde Societëit), Feb. 3, 2021, https://achurchdismantled.com/henk-stenvers-essay/.

leaders to guide the flock. And of course, with the formal bureaucracy gone, it is a less complicated job to care for that flock—fewer meetings to decide on the color of the carpet, to decide what time Sunday School will start, to plan worship services (which become less complicated), to fill positions on ballots, to design new programs, and on and on. For indeed, all that is left is the people of God, and for all intents and purposes the iron cage has become irrelevant.

We can bemoan the loss of that cage these days and the fact that it just might be that the U.S. Church is following the European model, or we can celebrate that we have finally been set free to be the people of God in the world that Jesus always intended for us to be. In other words, that the powers of Christendom have been broken, that the impacts of the Enlightenment have been minimized, and that the Spirit just might break out anew as a result.

Henk's description of the Dutch Church just leaves that hopeful door open, if only a crack! For what he accounts for that Weber did not, was a Spirit who existed long before the Enlightenment and modernity and who dismantles and disrupts whatever gets in the way of that highway to the new heaven and new earth.

CHAPTER 4

Why the Old Order Amish Are Not Spending Hours in Committee Meetings to Decide to Open the Church
July 2020

I don't know if you've thought about it, those of you who know anything about the Old Order Amish, but they are out in the fields, harvesting corn, working in the kitchen, building homes, having weddings and funerals, and living life pretty much as normal these days.

I teach a course at Elizabethtown College on the Old Order Amish, and I've always taught that in a time of economic crisis, a terrorist attack on our electrical grid, or an oil embargo that dried up the gas at our local convenience store, the Amish were the best prepared, since so much of their existence is off the grid already. But I never for the life of me thought that in a time of a spiritual crisis in this country that they would be ahead of the game. What with their no-nonsense piety (which lacks the emotion of the heart), their practice of shunning (which threatens to destroy the heart and the heart's relationships), and the demanding practices and expectations that come with life in a communal, religious society that was formed in the late 17th century, I assumed that we moderns who had been set free from such constraints and imprisonment would be the better off for it.

The problem is that I was wrong. At least in part. While most churches and their leaders are spending an inordinate number of hours deciding when, if, and how to reopen, regather, reassemble, and so on (often resulting in heated arguments), pastors threatening to resign, saints getting weary of waiting and heading to other churches that seem to have solved the problem for now, budgets declining, and in general any momentum a church had going down the tubes. . . . As I said, the Amish are milking their cows, picking flowers, walking down the road to church.

To church? Why, yes, of course. For all the talk these days of the novel idea of house churches and the amazing innovation they just might be, the Old Order Amish have been house churching for centuries. I do hear a lot of talk about house churches right now, and I have to say the idea has an appeal to me that it never did in the past. Perhaps that's just because I so long for the gathering of the saints, wherever it might be. Or perhaps it is because it is the house church model that kicked off the Church and that it will be the house church model that signifies the end of the Church as we have known it in modernity.

The thing is, I don't think it's as easy as it looks. The Amish house church model works because they've never been a people who have known themselves by the house they worship in or where they gather. For an Amish district containing thirty to thirty-five families, they *are* the church. There is no differentiation between place and people—they are the church and the church is them. They are the community, and the community is the church, and the church is the community. Talking about reopening the church would be nonsensical to their vocabulary and ecclesiology; the church of God can't be closed, because it is not a place. The Amish understand that they are the church, because they are not captured by all the rational questions of modern congregations.

More than one hundred years ago, Max Weber, a sociologist writing in Germany, argued that the modern world would eventually lead to an iron cage in which modern societies would find themselves captured by bureaucracy and red tape and regulation and policies and memos and all that which accompanies every bureaucracy. He warned that rationality would eventually become irrational.

Most of those who are sitting in church business meetings these days are probably beginning to get some sense of just how irrational we've made church, how lacking in organic and human realities, how bound to the larger environment in which it finds itself. So in touch with the earth. So out of touch with heaven. It would be great if the Amish would package and distribute a little guide to house churches about right now. The problem is that that would be a rational response and as moderns we would see it as a list of ten things to get your church back together again.

This is not a criticism of any congregation or its leaders—I am one of them. It is a recognition once again that the people of God got suckered by the modern world a long time ago and perhaps the best thing for us would be for the trappings of modernity to finally be stripped from the church. I don't know. But I am wondering.

CHAPTER 5

Pizza Camp, Yo-Yo Ma, and Those Cemeteries of Amateurs
June 2021

One of the activities that gives me great joy is listening to or watching those who, in my words, are "good at their trade or craft." These are folks who have honed their ability, often across decades of failure, experimenting, and following the guidance of that old adage, "If at first you don't succeed, try, try again!" I so enjoy speaking with folks for this podcast—speaking with folks who are humble about their accomplishments, but who once they begin to share, light up with a passion that pulls me along with them, who out of seemingly random experiences over time, have now discovered a path that has led to their success. And yet the truth is, so few of them describe themselves in terms of being successful, because for them, the joy of doing and of being in the midst of the doing always outweighs the price that someone is willing to pay for their efforts.

Several years ago, the summer that I was diagnosed with Parkinson's disease, Heidi gave me a copy of the book *Pizza Camp*, written by Joe Beddia.[12] Beddia owns a small pizzeria in Philadelphia that has defied all the odds of the restaurant industrial-complex, which has rules and norms for just how one can be successful in an industry where the odds are always against survival. At Pizza Beddia, Joe and

---

[12] Joe Beddia, *Pizza Camp* (New York: Abrams, 2017).

his one employee produce thirty pizzas a night for about thirty bucks each. There is no calling ahead, no ordering online, and no sitting down to eat. It is take-out only. The only way to get one of Joe's pizzas is to get in line, usually long before the shop opens at 5:00 p.m., and to wait in line, give your order, and then pick the pizza up several hours later. Be prepared for a late dinner. Clearly, Joe breaks the rules of McDonaldization. But Joe has had great success. His food has been named by *Bon Appetit* magazine the "Best Pizza in America."

I began baking pizza for our family as a kid, often riding my bike first to our Amish neighbors about a mile away to purchase the mozzarella cheese, then riding home and using a simple pizza dough recipe from an Amish cookbook: oil, warm water, yeast, salt, sugar, and flour. Kneading but no rising was required.

But Joe's recipe again, like his restaurant, defies what I had always understood about bread baking. Joe's recipe uses cold water, very very little yeast, and the dough is placed in the refrigerator for twenty-four hours before it is used. There is no kneading, but lots of time to rise. And lots of salt. And *Bon Appetit* is right: The outcome is by far a better pizza crust than any I've eaten anywhere. I say that with no credit to myself but all of it to Joe, who spent a year in Europe with the best pizza pie chefs. Joe is good at his trade. He's done the work for we amateurs who dabble in the mysteries of yeast. If you have a pizza stone, semolina flour, and a 550-degree oven, you too can bake the best pizza in America—hands down. But only because Joe Beddia shared his recipe; again, breaking the rules of success.

But Joe had learned the hard way. Growing up in Lancaster, Pennsylvania, he had lost his mother and suffered deeply as a result. He dropped out of college. He wandered. He studied wine for a while before he bounced to pizza. His was a zigzag journey.

Last weekend I watched an interview on PBS with Yo-Yo Ma, who has undoubtedly been the best cellist for decades. His fame began as early as the age of seven, when he played for President John F. Kennedy. Decades later, he helped many a person through the season of Covid with his beautiful album "Songs of Comfort."[13] But there is not an ounce of arrogance in Yo-Yo Ma. Indeed, he is spending these latter years of his career trying to bring a divided country together and to encourage the development of musical gifts among budding young musicians. Yo-Yo Ma bemoaned the tragedy of what he and the host described as that "cemetery of amateur musicians," where so many who began music lessons as children and even became pretty good at their trade, buried their talents and walked away from their passion. Why? Because, said Yo-Yo-Ma, "of the development of recordings." He noted that before we could record music, if we wanted to hear a piece we had to sing it or play it ourselves or spend time with other singing and playing folks. But professional recordings made us all consumers rather than players and participants. Thus the cemeteries and thus the lost gifts and so many who could have become really good at their trade.

In both of these examples I think of the Church and how we move forward after the dismantling and as part of the grand excavation project of Isaiah 40. What have we been doing that has been about following the rules of supposed success, passed down to us from a past in which those rules functioned well but in this moment of dismantling are now irrational, and can we now let go of those things? What have we picked up from the modern world and other social institutions that should never have been part of what it meant to be the people of God, and can we now let go of those things? To what degree have we absorbed the cultural fog of the last three hundred years of American culture, with its violence, systemic racism, personal independence, individualism, and syncretic faith that mixes God with country? The sense that bigger is always better and that mega-this and mega-that are

---

[13]   https://www.yo-yoma.com/sounds-symphonies-archive/songs-of-comfort-and-hope/.

the metrics of success? The sense that church services must be perfected within a forty-five minute window in which only the best get to sing and play and preach and teach? Where children are seen as consumers of religious products rather than collaborators and participants with us in lowering mountains, raising valleys, making rough places smooth, and crooked places straight?

Twenty years ago I assumed that answering these questions was my job and our job. But I am now convinced that the answers come only from a Spirit who is in the midst of offering answers and doing the work already, if only we will take the time to "be still and know that I am God." Any church meeting that begins without asking what the Spirit is saying and acknowledging that Christ is present, will never be a church that is able to break the rules needed to make the changes required in this dismantling season. For without such listening, we will see and hear only our own good ideas. And if that were good enough, then the change would have happened a long time ago.

While I sometimes grieve that I am living in this season of dismantling, I am also thrilled to be a collaborator in this grand break-up of rules and regulations that have guided the Church for too long. For it just might be that those of us living now get to witness and experience the Spirit breathing upon those dry bones of Ezekiel, and the final resurrection of that new heaven and new earth.

PART TWO

PASTORS IN
A PANDEMIC

CHAPTER 6

Pandemic Pastors and Just About Everyone Else on That Cliff Ledge
August 2020

Sleepless last night, I found myself listening to a variety of hymns and other songs that take me back to places and times when I was overlooking an abyss that terrified the living daylights out of me, but where I knew remaining on the ledge of the cliff was no longer an option. For example, the day in August 1990 when Heidi and I separated, and I had nothing but uncertainty in front of me as a single father—this was an abyss of terror if there ever was one. And yet I couldn't sit on the ledge for long—I had a son to care for and a doctorate degree to begin. Or the moment I was diagnosed with Parkinson's disease, that "all-encompassing illness," my family doctor said, "that I definitely did not want to have." But I couldn't remain in the doctor's office—I had life to live. And the many trips to various hospitals since 2000 for both Heidi and I related to our multiple diagnoses of various cancers, and follow-up appointments for which we awaited test results.

I always knew before we left the house for those trips to the hospital or the doctor's office that when we returned, the landscape of our lives could look very different—either returning with new hope for the future or returning to deal with more uncertain news, or, worst of all, to face the news that further treatment was hopeless. But we had to go get the news regardless. Good or bad, we couldn't sit in the driveway of our house forever, uncertain as we often were, and as we on so many days still remain. We moved forward, always putting, by God's grace, one foot in front of the other, even when doing so appeared to be leaving the security of the cliff ledge where we had hung out for so long and that for a season served God's purpose. But God always calls us onward and off that ledge.

But in this fall of 2020, as I consider this my fifty-second year of entering the classroom as either a student or a teacher, what lies ahead again seems rather abyss-like. Some of my students are attending remotely on Zoom, some are in the classroom socially distancing, some are coming in immediately, others a week later, and others two weeks later—and all the while, we know that Covid cases could send us all running for cover once again.

Yesterday Heidi and I returned from some time away, in which Christ gave us both some clarity about this cliff ledge we've been hanging out on at our church. After months of waiting to regather our congregation for services, I returned to announce that we would do so as a congregation the upcoming Sunday. We would reassemble to meet Jesus at the communion table once again after months of remote worship services and much debate and enough conflict to know that my doing so might only add fuel to the fire. The announcement I made created anxiety and concern even more than I anticipated. Despite repeated calls by some to "reopen" our church, when I moved ahead to do so, the call to move from the cliff ledge of the "closed church" created much more consternation among some of the saints than I had expected. It was a reminder that none of us move easily from where we are, even if we have expressed restlessness with where we are. The ledge seems so much safer than the jump from that ledge.

In so many ways for all of us, as the rituals we are accustomed to disappear in the midst of this pandemic, we are left torn between the terror and anxiety of longing for what was and the fear of moving from where we are, knowing that we can't go back again. What is in the rearview mirror is gone, and the headlights don't reveal enough of what is ahead to bring us any comfort. If we begin gathering as a congregation once again, what happens if we all get sent home again? What will our congregation do for gathering come winter? Maybe the church should just remain "closed" indefinitely. What should we do in such a moment?

For our congregation, this question seems parallel to the day Heidi drove away and I was left alone as a single father, the day I received the call that I had thyroid cancer at age thirty-five, the day I was called out of the classroom in 2008 to take a call from Heidi that she was being tested for ovarian cancer, and on and on. Each of these moments, as such moments have for you too, felt like looking over the edge of an abyss, and sometimes the terror we feel takes our breath away and the beating of our broken hearts seems to threaten to kill us.

And yet all of us, when we look back, made the choice to step off the ledge of the cliff eventually and to drop into the dark unknown, continuing life as a single father, leaving the doctor's office, going to the next appointment to hear the news (good or bad), knowing only that the God of Psalm 91 had promised that "...he will command his angels concerning you to guard you in all your ways... Those who love me, I will deliver; I will protect those who know my name. When they call to me, I will answer them; I will be with them in trouble, I will rescue them and honor them. With long life I will satisfy them, and show them my salvation" (Psalm 91:11, 14–16).

With Parkinson's disease these days, I am especially touched by how many such passages are in the Old Testament that assure us that God will not let our foot slip or that he will not let us fall. These promises were given to a people who daily traversed a landscape that threatened them, that included paths overlooking those terrifying abysses. They needed these promises from a God who protects those on the cliff's edge. And we need those promises just as much today.

I used to read passages like Psalm 91 about God protecting the saints from harm and wonder how that promise lined up with the suffering I knew some people experienced and that I would later experience myself. But I was measuring suffering from such a limited perspective and outside of God's eternal perspective in which that promise really stands—that despite pain, suffering, injustice, oppression, the resistance of others, etc.—we will really get home free finally safe and sound.

It's no wonder that among Jesus's last words were these to his disciples just before he left them, disciples who must have felt on the edge of an abyss in light of the confusion they were experiencing: Friends, said Jesus, "...remember, I am with you always, even to the end of the world."

And so whatever the abyss looks like in front of us, no matter how terrifying the uncertainty of "church" as it approaches, let's not forget those words once again: " I am with you always, even to the end of the world." And if he is with us until then, certainly, as I always tell dying saints, "Surely he will hold your hand as you cross that thin veil between here and the new heaven and new earth."

So whether we remain on the cliff ledge or by faith throw ourselves into the darkness in obedience to Jesus to do what he is asking of us next, the promise of Psalm 91 remains, "With long life I will satisfy him and show him my salvation." Long life indeed. Long, long life, with the cloud of witnesses cheering us on in this pandemic of uncertainty.

CHAPTER 7

Crying Pastors and Feuding Saints— but if the Spirit Is Dismantling the Church, It Should NOT Be Easy to Put It Back Together

July 2020

If you are a pastor these days, chances are pretty high that you have shed some tears, done some serious soul searching about just what Paul meant when he said that it is by God's mercy that we have this calling, and found yourself licking some new wounds that have appeared simultaneously with Covid. Because, as some friends of mine are prone to say, "I don't care who you are," there isn't anything easy about the mess we are in. If we thought doing church was hard prior to Covid, we hadn't seen anything yet. Those of us who were sick and tired of tradition just now may be wishing for a bit of tradition—because the thing about tradition is that you have it memorized and can do it sleepwalking without falling off a cliff. But if you are a church leader and go to sleep now (well, chances are you're not sleeping much these days anyway), it is hard to know how the world will have changed by the time you wake up.

The saints are not having an easy time of it either. Some of them, and perhaps many of them depending on the congregation, are locked in hand-to-hand combat as it were—defending the use of masks as well as the right to not wear masks, arguing over whether Dr. Fauci is the hero in this epidemic or the Antichrist, accepting everything the CDC puts out or trashing science, data, and technology (except for the science, data, and technology that keeps their channel news show going), and anything else they happen to be hanging onto for security these days.

I thought I was wise to ask our church board to make the decisions about reassembling our congregation. The board has worked tirelessly and faithfully, but at the end of the day it is not their responsibility to carry out the ministries of the church. As I approached the task ahead, I found myself overwhelmed and fighting back the tears. *Why? Am I alone?*

I'm pretty sure I'm not alone, and there is a good sociological reason for the emotions we are feeling and, of course, a good theological reason.

First, the sociology. Peter Berger, in what is now a classic book title *The Sacred Canopy*, describes the overarching canopy or cosmos that religion provides for us.[14] This canopy provides meaning for us and helps us to make sense of our world. Most of us are born within the confines of this religious covering, or we convert our way into it. It is an incredibly powerful force and provides at least two things: 1) Social interaction and engagement with others who believe as we do, who reinforce our beliefs and our faith in God, and 2) Moral direction for our lives and guidance to know what is right and what is wrong and what to believe or not believe. In other words, the sacred canopy offers safety and security—something we are born with a desire to have and without which we cannot survive as a human species.

Which brings us to the other side of Berger's argument. That when the sacred canopy is tattered or even disappears—we are left naked without social integration and without a moral compass. In other words, we will feel lost and disoriented, as if our home has been taken from us. In March of 2020, in so many ways it was.

---

[14]   Peter Berger, *The Sacred Canopy* (Garden City, New York: Doubleday, 1969).

The risk of losing our social and moral bearings is in fact quite serious. Berger, based on the work of Émile Durkheim in France in the late 19th and early 20th century, uses the word "anomie" to describe the loss of social integration and moral cohesion.[15] Berger says it is like looking over the edge of a cliff, and it is accompanied by the kind of fear such self-awareness brings us. When I think about doing ministry and essentially starting from scratch with no road map or old ways of doing things, I feel like I'm peering into a black hole. But if I didn't feel that way, I would not be facing reality.

As leaders it is important to keep in mind that the saints are finding it easier to fight over masks than to allow themselves to imagine that what we knew of church and church life is now gone. I mean, when will the CDC ever approve potlucks again? Will any of us ever really want to try Sister Ethel's tuna salad again? What appears to be feuding among the saints may be for some of them simply their way of coping—keeping them from looking over the edge of the abyss, which we as pastors have no choice really but to do.

Nothing in seminary prepared us for this. No amount of money will make this any easier. Yesterday in the middle of my day, this phrase suddenly swept through my head: *It's not supposed to be easy.* What isn't supposed to be easy? Putting the church back together again. Because if the Spirit is dismantling the church, any efforts we make to put things back in place in ways that simply make us feel better and less anxious and anomic are not likely to work out in the long run. Because the same Spirit who has dismantled the church is pretty apt, I suspect, to keep it dismantled until we are finally resolved to feeling the fear that comes from looking over the cliff and seeing nothing but darkness below.

Anomie is the loss of social integration and our moral com-

---

[15]   Émile Durkheim, *Suicide* (Originally published 1857; published in English by Routleldge and Kegan Paul, 1952).

pass. I'm pretty sure that's the context God's people found themselves in when Jeremiah penned these words to them as they were surrounded by their pagan enemies in Babylon:

> Thus says the Lord of hosts, the God of Israel, to all the exiles whom I have sent into exile from Jerusalem to Babylon: Build houses and live in them; plant gardens and eat what they produce. Take wives and have sons and daughters; take wives for your sons, and give your daughters in marriage, that they may bear sons and daughters; multiply there, and do not decrease. But seek the welfare of the city where I have sent you into exile, and pray to the Lord on its behalf, for in its welfare you will find your welfare." (Jeremiah 29:4–7)

The folks reading this letter for the first time had to believe that Jeremiah was out of his mind, until perhaps they remembered that he of all the prophets had been right about the whole being sent into exile thing, when every other prophet was prophesying just the opposite. In the end, the prophet is validated by God's reality and what really goes down, not by what others think of him or her. And what this prophet brought to God's people this time was, "You are on God's mission. You thought this was exile, but God has planted you here to bring God's reign and God's kingdom. Now get at it, before you miss out on that same kingdom that will find its way back to you, if in fact you offer it to your neighbors. And by the way, God says, before you jump over that cliff and end it all, I happen to have some plans for you, and regardless of what you might be feeling right now, they are actually plans to yet prosper you, to give you hope, and a future."

Those words right now might just be enough to back any of us off from the ledge of the cliff.

CHAPTER 8

What I Am Learning From My Students, With Lessons for the Church

February 2021

This week I began teaching for the spring semester again at Elizabethtown College, which is going all remote for at least three weeks. I think congregations that are struggling over whether to "reopen," whether to mask or not, whether to believe that Covid is real or not, could learn some important lessons from places like Elizabethtown College.

First, someone is in charge and has authority to make policies that are enforced, allowing us to get on with the mission. The administration required masks, so we did it. No bickering, no trying to get out of it, no sharp jabs at the President. Want to attend? Wear a mask. Want to teach? Wear a mask. Congregations have gotten lost during Covid and abandoned their mission because they are too busy challenging leaders over whether to return or not return, mask or not, etc. Covid has revealed again how little authority leaders have in the church. And as I've often said, where there is no authority, the mission will never get traction.

Second, the students have taken command of Zoom and are mastering it as a means to interact and communicate. They are much more confident and engaged than they were one year ago. I have three courses with about thirty-five students in each, and they were chatting alongside the margin of their laptop screen, and most had their screens open. Because they had no choice, they adapted successfully. Too many congregations are just waiting to get back to "in-person" gatherings rather than using this time to adapt to new ways of doing things that actually make the Church relevant. Social media technologies are as revolutionary as the printing press, and those that adapt will be far ahead of the game.

Third, my students emphasized that they are confident that the past is past and there is no going back. They experienced a "no-Covid" world, now a Covid world, and at some point, we trust, a "post-Covid" world. That world will not be like either of the other two, and their willingness to acknowledge this reality will help them to adapt and construct a new reality. But congregations that deny the reality of how Covid is changing the culture of the Church and world will be unable to adapt to what is coming.

Fourth, it is a waste of time to teach as if Covid and the social chaos around us is irrelevant or insignificant. I have largely abandoned my stock and standard teaching approach and am engaging students in the context of what they are experiencing. This is the richest time of my life for being a sociologist and studying society, and that is what we are doing together. What if congregations saw this as the richest time to bring Shalom to the world and that was our only focus as a Church? It would mean abandoning much of what we did pre-Covid and assessing everything going forward through the lens of our new reality. I continue to be amazed at the Church's capacity to keep plodding along, doing things that were scheduled a year ago, before Covid. But apparently we must show our value even when what we are showing up to do is no longer valuable!

Fifth, we share an agreed upon reality of science. By and large, we believe the data about Covid and disease. We believe the data about climate change. We believe that reality is still perceived through the five senses. I always tell my students that trusting the empirical method doesn't exclude other ways of knowing or experiences of the supernatural, but if we are going to learn together, we have to have some agreement about our methodology.

Sixth, students come to learn and not to check my teaching against their beliefs. They honor me as the one who can facilitate their learning and by and large trust that I am doing so. Such honor can be difficult to find in today's Church, when most leaders are considered suspect by the consumers in the pew who are listening to talk radio or watching their favorite cable news show. The editor of *Christianity Today*, once shared with me in a podcast, his awareness that, "Most pastors are one sermon away from losing half their people."[16] I thank God I am not held to that standard in the classroom!

---

[16]   Podcast interview (December 8, 2020) with Daniel Harrell for the podcast "A Church Dismantled—A Kingdom Restored."

CHAPTER 9

Another Lesson From My Students—
Frozen Cultures . . . Dying Cohorts
February 2021

I met with my students today on Zoom. There were thirty-six energetic faces all engaged in the topic of culture and the factors that bring about culture shock. I shared my own story of traveling to Ecuador at the age of twenty and living with a Quichua peasant family, and the terror I felt when I had convinced myself that they were going to force me to marry their daughter Marta and would never allow me to return to my home in Big Valley. Of course, that wasn't the case, but the terror was real.

The terror we feel when we change cultures, or when culture changes us (such as we are experiencing in this pandemic), comes from the disorientation we feel when the landscape of our culture changes. Sociologist Peter Berger describes the loss of norms or unwritten rules and the social isolation we feel when that occurs, as the experience of standing on a cliff, looking down into the abyss of nothingness.[17] Doing so creates tremendous anxiety, fear, and paralysis. As humans we are accustomed to fighting or fleeing when we are afraid, but fighting or fleeing on the edge of this Covid abyss just might take us over the edge. And so we freeze. And the Church by and large has frozen.

Why? Because we are old. I said this fifteen years ago in *Road Signs for the Journey*, my study of American churchgoers. Our kids

---

[17]   Peter Berger, *The Sacred Canopy* (New York: Doubleday, 1969).

are fleeing us, our average age is going up, we're having fewer kids, our rural neighborhoods are graying. And so we are slowly dying and freezing in place, just hoping after Covid we can get back to normal and back away from the cliff.

After this conversation with my students, I am thinking that we in the Church are simply afraid and quite honestly don't know what to do except what we've always done. Why? We of all people are those who follow the Author and Perfecter of our faith. The one who for the joy set before him endured the greatest of all abysses—the greatest abandonment. Folks, we have not been abandoned. This cliff is not where the story of the Church ends and certainly not where the story of the kingdom ends.

I'm reminded of King Hezekiah, who, when told by the prophet that the Babylonians would come and take Judah into exile after his death, because of his disobedience, breathed a big sigh of relief and said something like, "Thank God it will not happen in my lifetime."

The church was just hoping we could get though history without the exile, without liminality, without being marginalized, and without having to depend on our Lord to lead us off the cliff. But God wouldn't have it that way, nor should he have if he cares at all about any of us, the world, and the kingdom.

So here we are on the edge of the abyss, the church frozen, and my students so much younger, energetic, engaged, adapting, advocating, and ready for whatever the future brings. The cliff is much less frightening when you are young and your culture hasn't solidified. Hezekiah didn't care whether the temple was desecrated or not; he just didn't want to lose the cultural map he had lived in during his lifetime. And why do you think God waited forty years to allow his people to enter the promised land? Because the old cultural maps had to die and their carriers with them—they would have only led to resistance in entering that new land!

As a sociologist grad student, I worked closely with Dr. Glenn Firebaugh, an Evangelical and a terrific sociologist from Penn State. Glenn developed a sophisticated statistical model that showed pretty clearly that the most effective social and cultural change occurs only when we old people die off.

And of course it makes sense why—because we take our faithless and myopic maps with us, and our passing creates space for younger generations to get off the cliff. The problem for the Church is that so few of our youth want what the Church is offering them, and so much of the Church really doesn't want who our youth are and who they have become. And so again it is culture that divides us—not the gospel and not the kingdom and not Jesus.

I am blessed to regularly hang out with eighteen to twenty-one year olds at Elizabethtown College. I am most comfortable with them these days—churched, unchurched, dechurched, never churched, don't want to be churched, and on and on. Because I can and do still talk with them about Jesus, the kingdom, and the gospel. And that still makes sense to them even when the Church doesn't. And that's a cultural map where I feel most at home.

CHAPTER 10

Pastors Fleeing the Church
April 2021

I entitled one of my blog posts, "Dear American church attender . . . your pastor doesn't believe everything that you do and also believes some things you do not," I wrote:

> I know that I risk appearing self-serving, but keep in mind that I'm an old guy with Parkinson's disease and not much of a threat to anyone. I've also been in ministry long enough to have tenure, which at least in higher education means I've earned the right to speak my mind on behalf of my colleagues who don't yet have their permanent employment status. And so since my own sundown is within sight, I share this much less on behalf of myself and more so on behalf of the many pastors that I know of who are struggling these days and on behalf of those who are wondering whether sticking with their calling is God's mercy or God's curse.
>
> One of my early research interests dating back to my graduate school days was in the differences between clergy and church members in their views of racism during the Civil Rights era in this country. The data were clear—clergy overwhelmingly supported the Civil Rights movement and efforts to address racial injustice more so than did the person in the pew.
>
> But this should not come as much of a surprise. Those God called to lead throughout the scriptures and in church history have typically been at a different place than those they are leading

. . . if they had not been they would not have been leading but rather joining the flock in meandering wherever flocks go without a shepherd.

There are many reasons that shepherds have a different view of the field and reality than the flock they are called to serve and lead. They are awake praying when the flock is sleeping. They spend time discerning the dangers to the flock while the flock is enjoying the green grass where the shepherd just lead them. They place themselves more times than the sheep are aware between wolves and the flock, knowing that in doing so they risk their very lives and livelihoods. They have a view and perspective of the landscape that the Chief Shepherd gives to them that the sheep often don't have the advantage of seeing. As a result, their view is of the entire flock and not just a particular group of sheep in the flock. They are aware that their decisions and preaching are likely to offend just about any one of the sheep at any time, and yet they preach on because to not do so would be to abandon the calling for which he/she alone will give account before the Chief Shepherd.

Much of the time the perspective of pastors and that which God requires of them means they will be at different places than their flock—precisely because God has called them to be so. And if they depended for their direction on public opinion polls the flock would never leave the fold and would just as likely starve to death. The pastor is out ahead of the flock for good reason. He or she is watching to make sure the flock stays clear of danger and that the flock ends up in green pastures and still waters. But the danger for pastors these days may be less the wolves ahead and more so the sheep acting out their second amendment rights.

A recent response of a pastor to my podcast relayed this:

Thanks for your writing. Honestly, it isn't just young adults who are feeling the "mantledness" of the Church and for whom the "Christian" formula doesn't work. I could so easily walk away from the "Christian" Church that has shown itself so clearly this year . . . and I am a pastor! I am more convinced than ever that Jesus offers a different way than what so many churches proclaim. That is what keeps me in the Church. I find hope in the messy love of Jesus. Indeed "kindness, acceptance, caring, and empathy are a much greater expression of divinity than judgment and condemnation."

I have no doubt this dear pastor speaks for many these days— I am privy to a lot of conversations, which is a trust I do not take lightly or for granted. Pastors have been traumatized by the conflicts within which they have been caught over politics and the pandemic. I have heard estimates from more than one denomination that they anticipate the resignation of at least one-third of their pastors this year.

In Ephesians chapter 4, the apostle Paul says this: "The gifts he gave were that some would be apostles, some prophets, some evangelists, some pastors and teachers, to equip the saints for the work of ministry, for building up the body of Christ, until all of us come to the unity of the faith and of the knowledge of the Son of God, to maturity, to the measure of the full stature of Christ" (Ephesians 4:11–13).

What strikes me about this passage is how much the "equipping of the saints for the work of ministry" and the building up of the body of Christ and the reaching of unity, developing maturity, and "the measure of the full stature of Christ." depends upon the spiritual leaders of the body. But when those leaders are continually sabotaged, repeatedly challenged, their preaching is compared to theories that members hear on talk radio and social media, and their spiritual anointing is discredited—we can expect that the flock will be as unhealthy and lost and compromised as it currently is in this country.

And so who can blame shepherds for deciding that the cost of running for their life from lions outside the fold might be less than the cost of being beaten up by the sheep in the fold? Yes, shepherds are called by Jesus to protect the sheep, but I don't believe that Jesus expected the sheep to jeopardize their own health and protection by beating up the shepherd. It might be healthy for the sheep to understand that without the lead shepherd, they still have themselves to deal with.

Until there is serious repentance among the sheep, I doubt there is much chance the fleeing of lead shepherds will change. Then what will become of the sheep? I don't know—hopefully a revival meeting will break out.

PART THREE

PASTORS IN A
POLARIZED CHURCH

CHAPTER 11

Where I Was So Wrong About the Church
May 2021

Over the past fifteen years, I have endlessly repeated that, "Churches who become like the world disappear into that world." And then I added, "unless they take Jesus with them." But what I usually had in mind were what I called the progressive churches and denominations who seemed to have given up on the exclusiveness of Jesus's claims, who seemed to embrace the idea that "many roads lead to Jesus," and who had latched onto the work of the "historical Jesus" folks that had stripped Jesus of his divinity. I assumed that the progressive and mainline churches had a relatively short horizon. And much of this still appears true. I assumed that it was Evangelicals who would sustain their Christian witness and that it was amongst them where I was most at home. And then came 2020-2021, and suddenly that home built by the God of Hebrews 11 seems ever more appealing as the one place I know that I belong.

I had always assumed that among Evangelicals, at least, if not fundamentalists, I would find a group of folks who, when they entered the world, would do so with Jesus. This past year showed me to have been correct about that, especially at the insurrection of January 6 where Jesus was so well-represented—though how well can be debated. What I realized after 2020-2021 and the Evangelical fights over masking and CDC science, the combining of "faith, family, and firearms," the T-shirts stating "Trump is my President and Jesus is my

Lord," and the coming to age of the compromises between Evangelicals and political parties and politicians, was that while I didn't feel comfortable with what I perceived to be the abandonment of Jesus by progressives, I also felt no more comfortable with the Jesus of so many Evangelicals today who appears nothing like the Jesus I read about in the Gospels. I always thought it was Jesus who in the last days would say to some of us, "I never knew you." But today I find myself saying of this Jesus, "I never knew you!"

I had assumed that if we Evangelicals hunkered down and preached Jesus, we would remain faithful to him. But I had forgotten to take into consideration what my favorite sociologist Peter Berger says about passing on the faith from one generation to another. First, the Church or society must speak as one voice to our children—parents, teachers, preachers, friends, and social media must all pass on the same messages to our children. Even among the most sheltered of Evangelical families, their kids are hearing a multitude of voices and having to decide for themselves which to believe. Second, the Church must "keep the world at bay" and set appropriate and defining markers that differentiate the teachings of Jesus from those of the world. But this seems like a lost battle after decades of the Church being co-opted by politicians whose morality has become irrelevant to us as long as they promise to protect us. It is a kind of exchange by which we give you our allegiance to the Jesus of the Gospels in exchange for your allegiance to us. The problem is that we've just stripped away the Lordship of Christ and the defining characteristics of the cross, which is to submit and to surrender to the dismantling work of the Spirit, which is ultimately to die to self and to choose death rather than defense, to turn the other cheek rather than to turn against our enemies, to flee to the margins rather than demand our right to be in the middle. In other words, Evangelicals are doing no better a job of representing Jesus than are progressives.

An avid listener and reader for my book manuscript, sent me this incredibly powerful piece by T. Austin Sparks. He was born in the late nineteenth century, and, like Judson Cornwall, was another prophetic voice regarding the dismantling of the Church:[18]

> The apostle Paul and his companions who can be said to represent the church went by ship, and that to my mind represents all such manmade means employed by God for the reaching of His ends, to Rome. On the way while on the one side there seemed to be so much that was working in opposition and reverse and contradiction; on the other side it was a case of the stripping off of all the works of men. The ship did go to pieces, the man-made thing employed by the sovereignty of God to reach His ends. It was thrown away when His ends were in the way of realization.
>
> There are a lot of things made by men, and godly men at that, which the Lord makes use of, but they will go, e.g. places of meeting, institutions, societies, organizations: they are made by men, they are useful, they help toward God's end, but like the ship, they are but means to the end. You must not put all your faith in the ship; you must not ascribe final values to the place, the means, the instrument. We shall find that the Lord has not committed Himself to keep the means intact, to hold the instrument for eternity.
>
> It is His Church that He is after, which He is preserving, which is to come out alive; and on the way, the 'things' will have to go, they will have to be broken up, they cannot meet the full impact of the forces of evil in this terrific storm. The forces of evil are too much for anything made by man, but they are not the equal of what God has made: His Church will come out all right.

---

[18]   Judson Cornwall, *Freeway Under Construction* (New Jersey: Logos International, 1978).

Be careful that you do not put too much upon God's means, God's instrument, the ship. Keep your eye on God's real object. The framework of things may break up, but God's spiritual values will be eternally preserved. And let us not worry too much if God sees the time has come for the stripping off of things. They may have served a very good purpose and our hearts may be very much linked with them, with that place or that instrumentality; but if the Lord begins to break it up and take it from us, do not think everything of value is going. No, it is the spiritual values upon which our hearts must be set.[19]

Perhaps this is the central thesis of this entire past year of writing for me—that it is all about God and not about the ship. And that God's Spirit is destroying the ship, or at least allowing it to destroy itself.

Another listener and also reader of my book manuscript, shared this on Facebook in response to my last episode:

Thank you Conrad for your thoughts this morning. Regarding the question about "closing the doors and giving up," this past week my wife and I traveled out of town for a wedding and, as we frequently do, were exploring the town in which we stayed. One of the places where we spent some time was a church building that had been converted into a brewery. The building was well kept and obviously a former "house of God." It struck me while we were there, that it could well be there was more of God's Spirit and Shalom present in that building now than may have been in the past . . . . Closing the doors of a church building is not the same thing as giving up.

19   Austin Sparks, First published in *A Witness and A Testimony* magazine, Sept.-Oct. 1951, Vol. 29-5, https://www.austin-sparks.net/english/002119.html.

Amen. Amen. The Church throughout history has shown this to be true.

Which brings me to the final point Berger made about how to sustain a religious institution: by religious legitimation. Simply put, when our children ask, "Why, Mommy and Daddy?" our answer is, "Because God." It's hard for our kids to hear this when their parents instead respond, "Because the Church," or, "Because our favorite politician" or, "Because of faith, family, and firearms."

No, whether the Church survives in the world, regardless of its theology and practice and beliefs otherwise, depends completely on which Jesus it takes with it into the world. Whether our children remain faithful depends on the same choice that we make. But as Dutch Mennonite Church leader Henk Stenvers notes, there will always be a people of God, regardless of whether one or another denomination survives the current storm, or whether your congregation or mine does so.[20]

I have to admit I was also wrong about a lot of folks I assumed were progressives—they talk a lot more about the Jesus I see in the Gospels than I realized and in fact have taken that Jesus of the Gospels with them into the world after all.

I've gotten so many things wrong.

---

[20] Hank Stenvers, "Walking on Water," Part 1, "Concerning the Future of the Dutch Mennonites" (Algemene Doopsgezinde Societëit), Feb. 3, 2021, https://achurchdismantled.com/henk-stenvers-essay/.

CHAPTER 12

The Day the Saints Went
Marching Into Washington, D.C.
January 2021

Before I went to bed the evening of January 5, I got my first glimpse of what the next day might hold. It came in the form of a Facebook post from a friend who excitedly shared that he was part of a three-bus caravan making their way to Washington, D.C., for the next day's events. Hard as it was for me to imagine any thrill in being part of a caravan of saints driving through the night, I thought little of it and went to bed.

But the next day I realized, as so many of us did, that what some expected to be a rather typical day of reporting protests on Capitol Hill, would turn out to be the reporting of death and destruction and dismantling. And the saints would be counted among that crowd turned wild—red, white, and blue flags waving, with "Jesus" and "Jesus Saves" printed on flags among others proclaiming "Trump," "Make America Great," and "No More Bullshit." It was clear that the saints had made it to D.C. Kind of like when the saints made it to Jerusalem during the Crusades—flags with the cross flying above them, swords, and their witness to that cross utterly destroyed for centuries to come. We still live in the shadows of those Crusades, and last week reminded us of that.

I have engaged widely with Evangelicals and mainliners and have been influenced by many faith traditions, but try as I have, I can't for the life of me understand how the Gospels can be read without recognizing that the Jesus of those Gospels is nothing like the Jesus represented by the religious right these days. I will say I was grateful to see a letter signed by 230 faculty and staff from my alma mater, Wheaton College, condemning the attack at the U.S. Capitol and the "vicious lies, deplorable violence, white supremacy" and "blasphemous abuses of Christian symbols" witnessed that day.[21] And I keep thinking of the Lutheran church during the Third Reich, and the costs to Bonhoeffer and the Confessing Church for drawing a line in the sand at the cross, refusing to be co-opted by power and the corruption power always brings with it.

It's hard to understand how Jesus's prayer in John 17 for unity could ever possibly be fulfilled this side of the new heaven and earth. But perhaps that's the point of the new heaven and new earth—that because Jesus's prayer can't be fulfilled here and now, we long for it so expectantly, and the earth groans so much inwardly, for that day when the lion and lamb will lie down together and will be led by a little child.

It seems, however, that while Jesus aspires to our unity in that prayer before his crucifixion, he of all people understood the division and sword that his coming had brought and would continue to bring—not a sword for him or his followers to bear, but the swords that would fly because of the clarifying truth of the gospel.

In my reading this morning, the passage was Matthew 10, where this warning of the gospel's tendency to divide and clarify couldn't be more clear:

"Do not think that I have come to bring peace to the earth; I have not come to bring peace, but a sword. For I have come to set a man against his father, and a daughter against her mother, and a daughter-in-law against her mother-in-law; and one's foes will be

---

21   https://www.insidehighered.com/quicktakes/2021/01/15/wheaton-college-faculty-staff-condemn-capitol-attack

members of one's own household. Whoever loves father or mother more than me is not worthy of me; and whoever loves son or daughter more than me is not worthy of me; and whoever does not take up the cross and follow me is not worthy of me. Those who find their life will lose it, and those who lose their life for my sake will find it" (Matthew 10:34–39).

I never really understood this passage until this morning—that Jesus is a Divider-in-Chief—that the gospel he brings is so radical and so demanding and so countercultural that those who take it even a bit seriously are going to begin feeling pretty uncomfortable among those who do not, among those co-opted by power and drawn into the corruption that power always brings. It is likely that families and friendships and congregations in the U.S. have not been more divided and more opposed to each other since perhaps the Civil War. A retired minister, when I recently shared with him the division in the Church, said, "What's the conflict about? Same-sex marriage?" I said, "Friend, that conflict was nothing compared to what we are seeing in the Church today."

So we should not be surprised that swords are drawn in Jesus's name nor that the Church is dividing and being dismantled right in front of our eyes. If we consider Jesus's words, that's likely good news. For a church in which no one had eyes to see what is going on in front of them in this moment and to name it for what it is, would be a church unlikely to be around for our children's children—who, by the way, I keep thinking about this week. I keep thinking as I write, "What do I want Ezra, our little grandson, to know that Pappy said in response to the state of the Church these days?" When I think of it in those terms, I care less about the responses of others to what I'm writing. Because I'm writing for those who are to follow. I'm writing for those who are going to need even greater moral clarity than we need today. I'm writing for those who just may be as likely to be persecuted by the Church as the world someday. But then, for those of us who claim Anabaptism as our faith identity—that thought should be a bit like déjà vu.

Interestingly, even in the midst of Jesus's dark warning in Matthew 10, his eyes too are on the children as the chapter ends, saying that "whoever gives even a cup of cold water to one of these little ones in the name of a disciple—truly I tell you, none of these will lose their reward" (Matthew 10:42).

A cup of cold water for a little one in need, or a sword and flag to protect my power and privilege? We can't nuance this one, friends—we are with Jesus, or we are not. Truth still matters.

CHAPTER 13

On Left and Right, We Who Become
Like the World Disappear Into It
January 2021

I n 2007 I published *Road Signs for the Journey*, a book that offered a profile of one Anabaptist denomination that was struggling with so many of the same issues that most of the Church in the U.S. has been grappling with. In that book I used the writings of the prophet Jeremiah as a guide to offer light upon our contemporary context. I quoted the prophet's words in chapter 2, in which he speaks for Yahweh regarding the people: "What wrong did your ancestors find in me that they went far from me, and went after worthless things, and became worthless themselves? They did not say, "Where is the Lord"" (Jeremiah 2:5–6).

A frequent comment of mine in those days was that, "Churches that become like the world, disappear into that world," and in so saying I was largely critiquing the more progressive churches that had become entirely assimilated into American culture, the promise of the American dream, upward mobility, and so on. I argued that the pathway of these churches into the center of the culture was leading to a watering down of their commitment to Jesus' teachings, to orthodoxy in regard to biblical teaching, to a declining Evangelical witness to the world, and so on.

At the same time, I offered some critique of Evangelical churches, but I felt more confident in their capacity to retain a more orthodox commitment to the teachings of Jesus and scripture, and sensed at that time a greater likelihood of standing apart from the broader culture and a greater willingness to resist assimilation and worship of the idols of that culture.

I was wrong. The past few years have revealed that churches in the U.S., whether leaning left or right, progressive or traditionalist, mainline or Evangelical, are equally guilty of becoming what we have worshipped. And for that, I think it is fair to say that we are all being hauled into exile. But exile might just be the place where some of us finally come to our senses and affirm who we are as the people of God and thus who we are as the people of God's shalom and God's reign. It will take some sorting out to figure out who is who, but I for one want to be among those who abandon the idolatry we have been caught in, who reject our position of power, who look not to the princes and kings of this world for our hope. No, I want to be among those of Hebrews 11 who "...confessed that they were strangers and foreigners on the earth, for people who speak in this way make it clear that they are seeking a homeland... If they had been thinking of the land that they had left behind, they would have had opportunity to return. But as it is, they desire a better country, that is, a heavenly one. Therefore God is not ashamed to be called their God; indeed, he has prepared a city for them." (Hebrews 11:13–16)

How thankful I am that the country and the city for which we are on pilgrimage is not the United States of America nor its capitol, Washington, D.C. For those who are truly saints are marching in the opposite direction.

CHAPTER 14

Learning to Become a #5 Church While the World Goes to Hell
January 2021

I believe that keeping the day of our death in view sharpens our awareness of what is most important in life and what is really real and truly true. My diagnosis of Parkinson's disease has given me a view of the horizon ahead of me that has contributed to a transformation, even a re-conversion. It has caused me to reassess the landscape that lies ahead of me and to reevaluate how and with whom, and in doing what, I want to spend my days of health that remain. This has been an invaluable gift. Abraham Lincoln, invoked last evening in the halls of Congress following the insurrection at the Capitol building so as to make one think there had been a conversion among our congressional leaders, said something to the effect that the measure of our days is not their length but how we live them.

Following the insurrection in our nation's capital yesterday, it again became clear why a reminder of the day of our death has a way of sharpening our sense of what is most important and reminding us of our shared humanity. A good threat of dismantling or an actual dismantling itself may be just what is needed for the Church to get back to the mission of God. Yesterday's attempt to dismantle our democracy seemed, at least for a moment, to sharpen the senses of our congressional leaders as to what their shared mission is for the people they represent.

Finally, I have argued that the Church has bought into rational models of carrying out God's mission, which have trapped it in what German sociologist Max Weber, in the early twentieth century, eerily prophesied would become an iron cage from which the modern world could not escape.[22] I have suggested that the stuckness of the American Church, bogged down in its rational systems and structures, has lost its way and that the dismantling of that Church is the work of God's Spirit to free it from its captivity—words Luther used to describe the condition of the church five hundred years ago.[23]

For me, yesterday afternoon represented a surreal coming together of all these arguments I have been making. I had signed up for a webinar hosted by a nationally known organization, which promotes the multiplication of churches—certainly something that I support. But as I sat watching rioters storming the U.S. Capitol building on one screen and the group of us looking placidly at each other on the other screen, being challenged to become "number 5" churches (multiplying) rather than typical "number 3" churches (embracing the status quo), I couldn't but wonder again when the Church will come to understand that it is stuck in an iron cage of metrics and irrelevancy while the world is going to hell around us. The last thing I wanted to worry about was how to become a "number 5" leader in that moment. I almost took a photo of the two screens together—a Zoom call of nearly all middle-aged white men trying to focus on rational techniques for saving the world, while it is so clear to me these days that it is the Church itself that needs saved.

I wondered which screen reflected most what is going on in the world today and where I needed to be focusing my energies. Now, I no longer wonder. I will go to the screen where I see Jesus, and last I checked, I couldn't for the life of me find a place where Jesus called me to be a "number 5" leader or where Jesus was spend-

---

[22]   Max Weber, *The Protestant Ethic and the Spirit of Capitalism* (1904).
[23]   Martin Luther, *The Babylonian Captivity of the Church* (1520).

ing his time leading seminars to create "number 5" churches. As a sociologist trained in quantitative measures, I know a bit about the limitations of the metrics of such methods, and they lack humanity, compassion, kindness, grace, justice, mercy, and on and on.

If the dismantling of the Church destroys the illusion that fancy metrics will save us, that will be a good thing. But after yesterday I remain doubtful. If the dismantling of the Church brings us to our senses and loosens us from the co-optation by political powers, that would be a good thing. But after seeing red, white, and blue signs with Jesus's name displayed in large letters at the Capitol, I remain doubtful. If the dismantling of the Church causes us to abandon our boats and Zoom calls to join the mission of God to the world God so loved and so loves still, that would be a good thing. But after yesterday, I remain doubtful.

What I know is that I am part of a church that is going to give account for the deeds we have done and not done, and right now from my perspective, our account has a negative balance. May God have mercy on us.

CHAPTER 15

What I Missed Yesterday— a Third Screen Where God Is
January 2021

I n the previous chapter I shared about the incongruity of watching two screens at the same time—on the one an insurrection at the U.S. Capitol building and on the second a Zoom call where I was learning how to become a number 5 church. But what I missed, mesmerized as I was by the drama at the U.S. Capitol and bored by what felt like the irrelevance of the Zoom call, was the third screen. Yes, a third screen, where God was at work. I wonder if he was even aware of the other two screens. Oh, I know he is omniscient and knows all things, but what I really mean is: Did he care that much about what was happening on those other screens?

I began thinking about this later yesterday while spending some time in Psalm 46 with a group of friends, a psalm that I have kept going back to again and again over this past year. Here is what the psalmist wrote while clearly living in a world that must have felt much like our own right now:

> God is our refuge and strength, a very present help in trouble. Therefore we will not fear, though the earth should change, though the mountains shake in the heart of the sea; though its waters roar and foam, though the mountains tremble with its tumult. There is a river whose streams make glad the city of God, the holy habitation of the Most High. God

is in the midst of the city; it shall not be moved; God will
help it when the morning dawns. The nations are in an uproar, the kingdoms totter; he utters his voice, the earth melts.
The Lord of hosts is with us; the God of Jacob is our refuge.
Come, behold the works of the Lord; see what desolations he
has brought on the earth. He makes wars cease to the end of
the earth; he breaks the bow, and shatters the spear; he burns
the shields with fire. "Be still, and know that I am God! I am
exalted among the nations, I am exalted in the earth." The
Lord of hosts is with us; the God of Jacob is our refuge.

I sent this to our congregation on Wednesday evening as I
called for prayer.

But it was yesterday while reading this passage with some
friends when I heard God's invitation:

"Come . . . come and see what I have done . . . come see
the dismantling that I am doing . . . come watch my screen if
you want to see what is really real and truly true . . . because
while you were watching nations in an uproar and kingdoms
falling, I am over on this screen desolating wars, breaking bows,
and shattering spears and burning shields with fire. While you
are watching chaos on one screen, chaos endorsed by far too
many in the Church, and while you are feeling distracted and
bored on the other screen, wondering about the relevance of
trying to become a number five church, come, come, come
over here, my child, and see the grandeur of what I am up to
. . . a grand excavation project of lowering mountains and raising valleys, making rough places smooth and crooked places
straight, so that my glory can be revealed to you, to those on
both of those screens you are watching, and to the entire creation that I so loved and so love still.

But to do that, to hear me, to see what I am up to, child, you will need to leave that Zoom call and shut down that news show, get off the Internet, and be still and know that I am God, that I will be exalted among the nations and that I will be exalted in the earth. And then once you've gotten to know me and what I am up to in the Church, the world, and your life—then come join me in my screen and help me bring the kingdom to the chaos and irrelevance you were watching on those other screens. But don't think about trying until you have spent enough time with me to know me and have been silent enough to hear me, to hear my promises, to hear my love, to hear the sound of heaven come to earth proclaiming, "on earth peace among those whom he favors."

I'm coming Lord, I'm coming, I'm coming . . . leaving both screens behind me.

CHAPTER 16

Why Church Multiplication Might Be Working Against the Spirit
January 2021

I keep thinking of that church multiplication conference that I was part of last week and the split screen of the insurrection in Washington, D.C., on the one hand and the conversation about church planting and multiplication on the other. I noted in the previous chapters, the disconnect that I experienced in that moment. And yet, in every church meeting since then I have heard next to nothing about the implications for the Church of what we experienced on January 6.

Friends, the Church cannot go on as usual. This is no longer the status quo. This is not 2019 nor is it even 2020 in the Church or in the world. David Brooks' column this morning was titled "Trump Ignites a War within the Church," in which he describes case after case of conservative and/or charismatic church leaders repenting for their sins over the past week of believing Trump's lies and repeating them.[24] One of those leaders (who has received death threats) shared on Facebook: "I have been flabbergasted at the barrage of continued conspiracy theories being sent every minute our way and the pure hatred being unleashed. To my great heartache, I'm convinced parts of the prophetic/charismatic movement are far SICKER than I could have ever dreamed of."

---

[24]   David Brooks, "Trump Ignites a War with the Church," *New York Times,* January 14, 2021, https://www.nytimes.com/2021/01/14/opinion/trump-evangelicals.html.

I suspect the reason that I have heard so little about the implications of last week's insurrection grows out of the fear that saying something will divide the Church. This year hasn't accelerated the divide in the dismantled Church so much as it has revealed that the divide is greater than most of us had any idea.

But it's so hard for us to back away from the institutional efforts of the churches we've created. Who will pay our salaries? What if congregations stop supporting us? Indeed, so much of what I'm seeing these days is more about sustaining, preserving, and protecting the Church as we've socially constructed it than it is, I'm afraid, about listening and discerning what the Spirit is up to in the world and the Church today.

We all learned in third grade that multiplying any number by zero leads to zero. I am afraid that multiplying the current version of the American Church might be about like multiplying what Moses saw as he came down the mountain—a people singing and dancing after having sold their souls to a golden calf.

No, if working at multiplying this current expression of the Church in America is what the Church is going to be up to, then count me out. I am much more interested in joining those who are quietly at work multiplying the teachings of the One who spoke in Matthew chapters 5–7—teachings that reflect the coming kingdom, and not the current Church:

> Blessed are the poor in spirit, for theirs is the kingdom of heaven. Blessed are those who mourn, for they will be comforted. Blessed are the meek, for they will inherit the earth. Blessed are those who hunger and thirst for righteousness, for they will be filled. Blessed are the merciful, for they will receive mercy. Blessed are the pure in heart, for they will see God. Blessed are the peacemakers, for they will be called children of God. Blessed are those who are persecuted for righteousness'

sake, for theirs is the kingdom of heaven. Blessed are you when people revile you and persecute you and utter all kinds of evil against you falsely on my account. Rejoice and be glad, for your reward is great in heaven, for in the same way they persecuted the prophets who were before you (Matthew 5:4–12).

PART FOUR

PASTORS AND
PRODIGALS

Writing to the Diaspora . . . From Church, From Religion, From God, From Modernity, From Community, From Family, From Self, and From Home

August 2021

While podcasting in mid-2020 I began to recognize that I was writing for what I began to call the disaspora—those in exile, those who have fled where they were and haven't looked back, those who were rejected, kicked out, or who left before they could be rejected and kicked out. Sometimes we have fled our actual homes and places of growing up, but sometimes we have fled a host of other expectations and situations and have just kept running.

That is, we kept running until Covid brought this rat race we call the American dream to a nightmarish halt. Working from home, ordering groceries from our local grocery store, ordering scripts from a mail-in pharmacy, and ordering everything else from Amazon. I don't know about where you live, but every other vehicle on the road these days is in some form either an Amazon delivery vehicle or a Hertz rental van working on behalf of Amazon.

And we can't go anywhere or do anything that keeps us on the run from whatever it is we are running from. No professional sports to occupy our minds on television or in arenas, gyms, stadiums, etc. No trips to Broadway to escape the chaos we are running from. No international travel. No flights to interesting destinations. Not even church as a final alternative.

And so we have been forced to stay home. And the longer we are home the more I suspect that we have begun to think about where we came from, how we got here, and whether there is anything to wait for, plan for, look forward to, or even live for. In other words, we have been forced into a kind of sabbatical, retirement, or, in Old Testament biblical terms, a year of Jubilee in which the fields were to rest from production, justice was to be administered by allowing slaves to become free, fields and building purchased by the 1 percent had to go back to the 99 percent, and so on.

We know from historical records that the people of God, like we today, rarely put into practice the year of Jubilee. I suspect the allure of holding onto all they had accumulated over the forty-nine years since the last year of Jubilee was too much to overcome, and they really would have hated to have seen their slaves go free when they were so well taken care of by their wealthy land owners. No, things as we have created them are pretty good, and what a tragedy it would be if we interrupted our great success by doing what is required of us: to act justly and to love mercy and to walk humbly with our God.

What an unfortunate place the world would be if we actually embraced justice and equality and equity and if we showed extraordinary mercy and kindness and love to both stranger and friend as well as to foe. What an interruption it would be to our busy lives to have to slow down and walk with the God of the universe, who, as St. Paul said, has a love for us that is wider and higher and deeper and longer than we have had any idea, that God who is able to do immeasurably more than we can ever think or imagine, that God who is constantly at work to see that all things work together for good to those who love him, that God who is invariably running after us to find us in the dark and despair of the rat race existence that we have lived, if living is even what it was.

Perhaps this is just in fact God's year of Jubilee. And perhaps it is just the time for all of us on the run, the diaspora of modernity, to listen for God's voice anew.

CHAPTER 18

Fleeing the Church to Escape the Devil— Only to Fall Into Jesus' Arms
April 2021

There is a lot that disturbs me about much of the Church these days. I don't know if it's just me and a new perspective of the Church or if it's the Church and its reaction to the recent political loss it perceives to have experienced. But wherever I look these days, I see a church in retrenchment and on the defense, hunkering down and retreating into a kind of irrelevance and self-protection reminiscent of previous periods when the Church feared marginalization and the dangers of a world that God so loved and that God so loves still.

Jesus didn't come to a welcoming world, a friendly world, a world ready to receive him. Jesus didn't enter a "church" ready for him or a "church" that ever accepted the message that he was sent to offer them. In fact, it would be that "church" that would facilitate his death—a death no more deserved than any person's ever was. And yet time and again Jesus spoke out against that church because of many of the qualities seen in the contemporary white Evangelical Church today.

I recently saw an image—a meme--on Facebook of a zebra being chased by a lion, with the herd of remaining zebras standing forlornly watching in the background.[25] The caption read, "This is

---

[25] https://achurchdismantled.com/f/the-mission-and-death-of-mj-sharp-and-that-little-zebra-again.

what happens to a 'Christian' who leaves the Church." It was an arrogant illustration suggesting that those who leave the Church will become the prey of the enemy. It was a way of wishing ill on those who for whatever reason felt a need to wander off from the herd, a way of smirking at those who sensed there just might be something more than what the Church was offering.

But it turns out that zebras do not leave their herd except under one condition. The only zebra who runs from the herd is the stallion, and he only does so when predators approach the herd. His running is obviously a way of diverting the enemy from destroying the others.

My response to the Facebook image was that it reminded me of the Lion of the Tribe of Judah, who chases down the very last sheep, just as the Shepherd goes out looking for that last little lost sheep, until he wraps it in his arms and carries it home. He says to that little sheep and the others who stayed behind that "there is greater joy in heaven" when one is found than when 99 of them hang out drinking Coke and watching TV and gossiping about that backslidden one for whom the Shepherd had to risk life and limb.

What such saints miss is that the Shepherd came precisely in order to lose life and limb for those who run away from the Church. I have classrooms full of such students these days—students whose parents left the Church or students who themselves left the Church. Some are straight, some are LGBTQ+, some are living a pretty good life, some are off in left field, lost and looking for hope. Sometimes their parents write to me to thank me for loving their child, for praying for them, for showing Jesus to them, for not rejecting them, for offering them hope. For I might be the only voice of Jesus they listen to right now, or even the last one they will consider before they write Jesus off altogether.

The last thing I would consider doing would be to show them that illustration of a lone zebra on the run from a lion. Instead I will show them the painting that Heidi has in our church office: of a Shepherd walking among a flock of sheep, holding one in his arms. That one he rescued from the lion, that one who left the Church because the Church didn't understand, that one whom Church leaders abused, that one who those in youth group taunted, that one of color who the white sheep told "just get over it," but that one that Jesus never lost sight of and never stopped chasing down.

Oh, parent of that wandering child, rest assured that the lion after your child has no chance against the Shepherd who already gave life and limb to find that child—and find that child he will. And I will look with him, even if I have to leave the Church with him to seek and to save the lost. By posting images like this one on Facebook, the Church seems to be feeling okay about itself. But most days I'm not at all sure that that is the case.

CHAPTER 19

Fleeing From the Church for the Prodigal— Finding God's Love for Me
April 2021

I love the idea from author and mystic Simone Weil, that sin is not "missing the mark" as I have so long been taught, but rather simply turning my face away from Jesus. I previously noted my lifelong anxiety about hitting that mark, about being good enough, about my chronic guilt and shame as I always fell outside the center of the target. Consumed by that shame, I tried even harder. I often wondered why we Christians were bothering to pretend that we had any good news to share with others when we, or at least I, hadn't a clue as to what that good news was.

But I have learned that the good news was praying my father-in-law, wayward as his life had been, into the presence of Jesus in the last hours of his life. It was finding in Mark, my strange but wonderful neighbor who claimed only a distant association with Christianity, who called me in the middle of the night before I was made a pastoral candidate, to tell me that I was the man for the job and that he was praying for me. It was my neighbor Cliff, who told me to get "the hell off" his front porch but then allowed me to lead him to Jesus, after which he found peace in restoring broken relationships. It was these folks, these zebras who had left the fold who actually led me, a supposed saint of the fold, to Jesus.

I had it so wrong. It was the prodigals who led me home, not the oldest sons or daughters. It was the prodigals who taught me that I was as broken as they were, or rather who made it safe for me to acknowledge my brokenness. It was and remains in the world so often that I see and experience the evidence of God's goodness and grace and compassion and acceptance, more so than is sometimes true in the Church.

This is why I reacted so strongly to the meme of a lion chasing a zebra with the tagline that, "This is what happens to Christians who don't need the Church."[26] More than anything, I grieved—because I hear from so many who had to leave the Church, and who in doing so just might have a greater chance of hearing Jesus and running into the Savior's arms. And if one looks closely at the photo, this is just a young zebra that is being chased down and is about to be torn to pieces. How can this possibly be good news? Do you have any idea how many parents share with me their pain regarding their children who cannot seem to find relevance in the Church? The question I am asking these days is not, how do we get our kids back into the fold, but who among us is willing to leave the fold to hang out with our kids wherever they are and whatever their identity? I am filled with grief these days.

As I observe the broader Church in this post-Covid world, a Church that perceives itself to have lost the presidential election or had it stolen from them, I fear a Church that is in retrenchment, that is reconsidering the cost of the mission of God, that believes the lies that we are safer from the devil within than without the Church, and that just might hunker down for another four years until we see whether the "right" presidential candidate wins the 2024 election.

I've been working with one particular church over the last few years and was encouraged by their movement toward God's mission. But in recent weeks I'm observing a reclaiming of an old "bunkering"

---

[26]   https://achurchdismantled.com/f/the-mission-and-death-of-mj-sharp-and-that-little-zebra-again.

and "fortressing" viewpoint of the past that damns the world rather than seeking its salvation, that declares greater dangers without the Church than within it, and that is likely more comfortable with the meme of the lost zebra being chased by a lion than one of a lost lamb being chased by the hound of heaven. I don't know for sure, but their rhetoric gives me pause.

Friends, we are called into the world. There we will not only find Jesus, but we also will find Jesus finding us. And we will discover for the first time perhaps that if God could love the prodigal, God just might also love me more than I had any idea. But we might need to leave our bunkers and our fortresses to discover this.

CHAPTER 20

Youth Fleeing a Church Dismantled— Just What Might They Be Seeing?
April 2021

I'm teaching my course on the Old Order Amish once again this semester, and we're reading two excellent books by Ira Wagler, who was formerly Amish and who describes his tortured journey of leaving his Amish community multiple times before he finally said goodbye for the last time. In discussing this with my students, one of them in passing noted that the Amish "formula" just doesn't work for every Amish person.[27] That was a keen insight that I grabbed onto and haven't stopped processing.

For we are all dropped into a cultural, social, spiritual map in which we are told what is right and wrong, good and bad, lovely and ugly, tasteful and disgusting—you get the picture. And for most of us, because conformity is more likely than deviance among human beings, we internalize most of what we hear and see. And we become like those who spent eighteen years training us. But not all of us.

Ten to fifteen percent of Amish youth, depending on the settlement, eventually choose to leave the Old Order Church. And the consequences and costs are typically high—for the defying of the social controls that keep them connected are usually controls that harm the heart and soul more than anything else. So why do they leave?

In my student's words, the Amish formula doesn't work for

---

27   Ira Wagler, *Growing up Amish* (Tyndale House, 2011).

them. Or in terms of a dismantled church that I described yesterday, somewhere along the line they came to recognize that the truth was "mantled" over it; it was covered up. The world they were given, over time no longer made sense to them, for they saw other realities. The everyday world that was comforting for others no longer brought them comfort. The answers provided for others no longer were their answers, and those that made sense to others no longer made sense to them. In sociological terms, the norms were no longer their norms.

Coming to the realization of this can be uncomfortable at the beginning, but tortuous over the long haul. Sociologists have a term for this experience: anomie. This occurs when the norms no longer make sense to us and when in that process we find ourselves suddenly alone. Normlessness and alienation—Berger says these two experiences are akin to standing on the edge of a cliff, looking into an abyss, and feeling sheer terror.

And so the choices for someone on that edge are either to jump into the unknown or to turn back and live your life in denial, even though it doesn't make sense to you, because you know how to perform and pretend like a character in a play.

Today's Evangelical youth are fleeing the Church. According to an article in this month's *Christianity Today*, those who are staying are often choosing to cohabitate, engage in premarital sexual activity, and likely other behaviors that the Church has historically frowned upon.[28] The part of that article that bothered me the most was the sheer lack of understanding of the power of the culture that our youth are growing up in and how that culture, much more than the teaching of the Church, has now been internalized. As Christian Smith and his colleagues point out in *Lost in Transition* (his excellent study of emerging adults), our kids are only acting out of the

---

[28]   David J. Ayers, "The Cohabitation Dilemma Comes For America's Pastors," *Christianity Today*, March 16, 2021.

faith they got from their Evangelical parents and their Evangelical churches.[29] Oh, we can blame our kids, but we are the ones who taught them so well.

We've given them difficult choices: leave, because the world we've given them doesn't make sense to them in the culture in which they live; or stay, and expect to hear us try to straighten them out after we have missed their first eighteen years to really show them the truth of the Jesus message, or invite them to stay and pretend like so many of the rest of us are doing.

And this, friends, is why I feel so strongly a call at this time in my life to dismantle the Church, because after teaching emerging adults for nearly thirty years, I understand what they are seeing better than I would otherwise. Also, after fifty-six years of my own life, I have come to new terms with my own recognition of how "mantled" the Church has become and how we have completely covered up Jesus in the process.

Maybe what some of our kids are actually hearing as they leave is an invitation from Jesus to experience freedom, joy, and life, which the Church had mantled up. I don't know. I only know that I want to be with them wherever they are hanging out when they leave the Church. Because what I've found after fifty-six years I'd sure like to keep sharing with them, and thank God I continue to have that chance. After all, a bit of kindness, acceptance, caring, and empathy is a much greater expression of divinity than judgment and condemnation. If you disagree with me, lay down the remote and reread the Gospels.

---

[29] Kari Kristofferson, Christian Smith, Hilary Davis, *Lost in Transition* (England: Oxford University Press, 2011).

CHAPTER 21

Still Fleeing the Church and Thoughts on a Long History of Doing So
April 2021

Today is the anniversary of the day that Dietrich Bonhoeffer gave his life for a cause that he considered righteous: the assassination of Adolf Hitler. Interestingly, Bonhoeffer had to flee a church that had been co-opted by the Third Reich and which Bonhoeffer was forced to reject. With others, he initiated the Confessing Church and an underground seminary to mentor leaders with a similar conscience about the annihilation of Jews, those with disabilities, gay and lesbian individuals, and others deemed "unfit" to carry on the purity of the Aryan race.

Centuries earlier, Martin Luther had also, though less intentionally, fled a church that likewise had been co-opted by the principalities and powers of the Roman state. He protested by nailing his statement to the doors of the Wittenberg church and initiated a flight from the church that continues to this day. But few of us who are products of that Reformation would wish to return to the Church of the Middle Ages.

In my own tradition of Anabaptism, the flight to find freedom from what Luther himself called the "captivity of the church" continued, as Conrad Grebel, Felix Manz, and others asserted their autonomy against those Reformers who had not left enough of the world behind them. The apostle Paul himself fled the "church" of his day, meeting Jesus, who called him out of darkness into light.

We could go on and on and on. Desert fathers who, in escaping to the cliffs and mountains to nurture a deeper life with God, also left a church behind. And in fact it would be the development of the monastic movement that would salvage the medieval Church and the written scriptures.

I recently wrote a little essay that got a lot of attention. I responded to a Facebook meme that displayed a zebra and a lion, with the lion chasing a zebra that had left a herd of other zebras behind. The meme suggested that this is what happens to church members who leave the church behind them. But what if the meme actually represents Jesus. In the meme of the lion and the zebra, was the lion actually Jesus chasing down a wandering saint or sinner? (Most days there is so little difference between the two.) Or was the lion the devil, pursuing a backslidden and wayward zebra foal that by looking to the world for a good time, found itself in the devil's sights? As I noted, I have trouble with what feels to me like churchy smugness and arrogance with this alternative rather than honest recognition that the devil is as likely to be in the fold as out of it; Jesus warned of this, in fact.

There are other ways of considering this meme. One of these includes the examples I began this essay with: those called to leave the Church of their day because it had become so corrupt, so co-opted, so converted to the world that it had lost its way. And those like Bonhoeffer, Luther, Grebel, and so many more who chose to cut their losses in order to save their souls.

In the midst of each of these situations, there were always detractors, critics, and a host of commentators. But in the end, each knew that they were accountable to just One on the day of their death. As Bonhoeffer stated on the way to his death: "This is the end—for me the beginning of life."[30]

---

[30]   https://www.history.com/this-day-in-history/defiant-theologian-dietrich-bonhoeffer-is-hanged.

I wonder, as I get emails and messages from so many folks these days who read and listen to what I'm writing, if some of their reasons for fleeing the Church are not in fact not that far removed from those I've just described, and if this flight for some isn't perhaps the only way to their soul's renewal and a new and likely first discovery of a God who loves them just as they are! That they are leaving the Church might be the first step towards finding their rest in the arms of a loving God whose power, presence, and grace are not restricted to the Church.

PART FIVE

PASTORS AS PROPHETS

CHAPTER 22

The Problem With Prophets—
the Problem With Jesus
March 2021

Jesus began his ministry by making clear just what he was up to: "The Spirit of the Lord is upon me, because he has anointed me to bring good news to the poor. He has sent me to proclaim release to the captives and recovery of sight to the blind, to let the oppressed go free, to proclaim the year of the Lord's favor." (Luke 4:18–19)

This is great news, unless of course you and I can't be counted among the poor, the imprisoned, the blind, the oppressed, and those slaves slated to be set free in the year of Jubilee. The question for us then is where exactly do we fit in Jesus' project to the world? For we have tried so hard to be among those with social status, to be those who are free, to be those who can see—to be honored, esteemed, and recognized—there doesn't seem to be much space for us in Jesus' agenda.

As a result, it doesn't take long for us to start muttering, "Isn't this just Joseph and Mary's boy? Didn't he grow up over on Walnut Street? Wasn't he the strange one, always a little odd? Wasn't his father just a carpenter? And didn't his parents begin their marriage in scandal?"

Jesus quickly responded and responds to us still: "No prophet is accepted in his hometown." But why not Jesus? Because the home-town folks always have a way of domesticating the prophet, of trying to keep them in their place, in that socially designated space that we have carved out just for them. Because if they begin to move out of that space, if they begin to change, who knows what will be required of the rest of us? And who knows who else just might rise up and declare themselves a prophet? The entire social system is at risk. No, it is always better to keep the hometown prophet in their place, or better yet, to throw them off the edge of a hill.

Sociologists note that social reality operates at two levels: first, the macro level of social institutions such as the economy, criminal justice system, religion, politics/government, health care, media, and so on. But these institutions also press down upon the micro level of our worlds of family, neighborhood, work, and ultimately self.

The problem with the hometown prophet is that they know their hometown too well, and everything they say is heard by the hometowners as a personal affront, as condemnation, as criticism, and as judgment. You and I can hear the words of an outsider without feeling threatened, but when our neighbor Cecilia, or Jose, or George steps out of line—well, then it threatens everything we have taken for granted about our world and about ourselves.

In a great book that Heidi and I are reading by Tod Bolsinger titled *Tempered Resilience: How Leaders are Formed in the Crucible of Change*, Bolsinger distinguishes managers from leaders. The church loves managers. It also says it loves leaders until, well, they begin to lead—because leadership requires change. And change always means loss. For most of us, loss is seen as dangerous and risky and unsafe. It's not long until we start looking for a hill to throw them from. As Bolsinger says, they are nearly always "sabotaged."[31]

Do we understand what we say when we declare Jesus is Lord? That we are opening ourselves up to danger, to risk, and to insecurity? Or have we domesticated Jesus as just a neighbor down the street—muttering the right words about him this Lenten sea-

---

[31]   Tod Bolsinger, *Tempered Resilience* (Downers Grove: InterVarsity Press, 2020).

son, but failing to truly submit to the deep change that he wants to bring to us?

I have long loved this prayer by nineteenth century Scottish author George MacDonald: "For thou art making me, I thank thee, Sire. What thou has done and doest, thou knowest well; And I will help thee: gently in thy fire I will lie burning; on thy potter's wheel I will whirl patient, though my brain should reel; Thy grace shall be enough my grief to quell, And growing strength perfect through weakness dire."[32]

Dangerous stuff, the crucible, the potter's wheel. But for the one who truly calls this prophet Lord, the only place to be. And for all of us, the very safest place to be.

---

[32]   George MacDonald, *The Diary of an Old Soul* (1880).

CHAPTER 23

Hometown Prophets Know Too Damn Much About Us
March 2021

I n Luke 4, Jesus spoke to the fact that hometown prophets are rarely accepted. I suggested in the previous chapter that it was because they are too familiar to the hometowners, too well known to assume anything divine could actually dwell within them, too much of the earth to be truthtellers from the heavenlies. And so Jesus, and later St. Paul, would abandon the hometowners for the outsiders, the marginalized, the down and outers.

But I also wonder if hometown prophets aren't most often rejected, not just because they are known so well to others, but also because they know the others so well. Jesus could see into the hearts of the Pharisees not only because he was divine, but also because he had grown up with them. For goodness' sake, he had been their teacher since the age of twelve! His ability to speak truth humored them then, but sounded a whole lot more real when he was thirty and said this in Matthew 23: 23–36:

> Woe to you, scribes and Pharisees, hypocrites! For you tithe mint, dill, and cummin, and have neglected the weightier matters of the law: justice and mercy and faith. It is these you ought to have practiced without neglecting the others. You blind guides! You strain out a gnat but swallow a camel! Woe to you, scribes and Pharisees, hypocrites! For you clean the outside of the cup and of the plate, but inside they are full of greed and self-indul-

gence. You blind Pharisees! First clean the inside of the cup, so that the outside also may become clean. Woe to you, scribes and Pharisees, hypocrites! For you are like whitewashed tombs, which on the outside look beautiful, but inside they are full of the bones of the dead and of all kinds of filth. So you also on the outside look righteous to others, but inside you are full of hypocrisy and lawlessness. Woe to you, scribes and Pharisees, hypocrites! For you build the tombs of the prophets and decorate the graves of the righteous, and you say, "If we had lived in the days of our ancestors, we would not have taken part with them in shedding the blood of the prophets." Thus you testify against yourselves that you are descendants of those who murdered the prophets. Fill up, then, the measure of your ancestors. You snakes, you brood of vipers! How can you escape being sentenced to hell?

Suddenly the truth hurt. Suddenly the bright little kid from the temple himself appeared as darkness. Suddenly this hometown prophet knew too damn much about the hometowners—because what he knew was what damned them.

But if only they had understood that he spoke the truth—for that truth would have set them free. If only they had recognized how sick they were—for then they could have been healed. If only they had embraced their blindness—for then they would have been given sight. If only they had recognized the bars that bound them—for then they could have been pardoned. If only they had recognized how wretched they were—for then they could have been made clean. If only they . . . and if only we the same.

The good news is that Christ remains at the door of our hearts . . . just quietly waiting until we finally get it. That with this prophet, the truth that damns us is actually spoken by the Truth who would still save us.

"Behold, I stand at the door and knock . . . "

CHAPTER 24

The Prophet Who Divides
Then and Divides Still
March 2021

I
t is an amazingly simple reality: "Let anyone who is thirsty come
to me, and the one who belives in me drink. As the scripture has
said, 'Out of the believer's heart shall flow rivers of living water"
(John 7:38). Living water, fresh water, life-giving water. Those who
believe in this One, from them will flow "rivers of living water."

Sociologists have a saying that is borrowed from others, but
which we apply to statistical analysis: "Garbage in, garbage out." The
software programs we use will analyze and give answers to anything
that we throw at them, as long as what we throw is numerical. In-
dicating truth or not is beside the point; the software knows how to
throw out whatever we feed it. And then we can parrot the output as
truth. And sometimes no one ever knows the difference.

But Jesus made things simple: "The truth will set you free."
And, "Whoever believes in me," from them "rivers of living water"
will flow. Fresh water, life-giving water, water in abundance. Jesus
knew that the human soul that "panted" for its Creator, that was
born to worship that Creator, would be able to distinguish living
water from bitter, from salty, from brackish. For living water gives
life, it nourishes, it heals, it quenches, it is enough.

And some will receive that water and some will not. John 7
records that some responded to this simple message, believing that
indeed Jesus was the "Prophet" or the "Christ." They were undoubt-

edly the simpleminded ones, the children, the marginalized, the unsophisticated who didn't know better except to know living water when they tasted it. Everyone else spent the day debating whether this One was capable of bringing forth such living water. He hadn't come from the correct place, he wasn't from the right people, and, for them, those facts alone were enough to wish him dead.

How can living water be so divisive, so readily discerned as living among those who've known everything except life, but received with such bitterness, anger, and hatred by those who all their lives have been reading about that water, have been preparing to receive that water, are from the right place, and in fact believe themselves to be the right people?

Rightness too often has this way of deadening our taste to that which is living.

CHAPTER 25

A Half-Crazed Preacher, a Grieving God, and a People "Prone to Wander"
June 2020

Over the past few weeks, I've become more aware of the love of God for me than ever before in my life, though this has been a kind of conversion that dates back to my diagnosis of Parkinson's disease. Somehow, strangely enough, I had to recognize my mortality and my limited horizon of good health, before I could become more open to the God who had created and loves me so—and you too.

But it's right in front of us, folks, all through the Bible, with scriptures like Ephesians 3, where our mystic friend Paul writes that the church at Ephesus would "have the power to comprehend, with all the saints, what is the breadth and length and height and depth, and to know the love of Christ that surpasses knowledge, so that you may be filled with all the fullness of God (Ephesians 3:18–19). Power to know God's love? Sounds awfully strange. We want power to do things, to overcome things, to achieve things, to carry out amazing miracles, to build things, to speak in tongues, and to give prophetic words. We want power to impress. But power to know God's love? You mean I don't just naturally allow myself to experience God's love? You mean I need God's power to help me to receive God's love? Yes, I think so.

Years ago our church had a preacher named Bud (Walter) Keener. Walter had an out-of-body experience as it were with the

Holy Spirit, which forever changed him, his view of God, his preaching, and just about everything about Walter.

Walter was attending our congregation when Heidi and I were in ministry from 2000-2005, and I used to shudder a bit when Walter stood up to share during the service—because one never knew what would come out of his mouth! Oh, he was never theologically incorrect to my knowledge, or rude or unkind or disrespectful; he was just crazy! Crazed by a view of what was to come that the rest of us did not have; crazed by experiences with God that we could only listen to but not really comprehend; crazed by the fact that we couldn't seem to comprehend what he saw; and crazed by the limitations of human experience when he had seen into the heavenlies. He tried as best he could in that skinny and increasingly frail body to coach the rest of us into those heavenlies, but I think looking back that he probably felt like he was on a losing team, and with a lead pastor at the lead who also had little clue of the heavenly mysteries that Walter had seen.

For all my anxieties about Walter, I knew one thing—the man was free and he didn't care what anyone else thought. And another thing: Walter was fully alive—one could never doubt that. Walter loved and trusted the God who had met him in the back forty during one of the early waves of the charismatic movement that swept through Lancaster County in the 1950s.

This past Sunday I preached a message from Jeremiah 3, where God is clearly grieving. Grieving a people who are prone to wander and have been so since the Garden of Eden. What was God to do? He would give his people the good life, but it was never enough. They had to try what was on the other side—even if "Death" in bold letters was clearly on that other side.

"I thought how I would set you among my children, and give you a pleasant land, the most beautiful heritage of all the nations. And

I thought you would call me, My Father, and would not turn from following me" (Jeremiah 3:19). God grieves. "I thought if I gave you what you want and need, if I held you in my womb (which is Hebrew for God's compassion) and gave you the safest and most secure place possible, if I defended you from your enemies, that you would call me father." But, alas, this has not been our proneness—to call God our father. Our proneness has been to run from him not just when he turns his head but in the broad daylight, as if to dare the Almighty from keeping us running headlong into death. But headlong into death he will allow us to go, not because he doesn't love us, but because he loves us too much to force us to love him back. For God, the gift of freedom that he has given to us is part of the package of love he offers us.

But what pain this has caused God. He offers us everything we need and want, but it doesn't keep us by his side. He draws lines in the sand to keep us near him, but for us any line in the sand is one to cross regardless of the cost. God woos us, and we wander.

In my message on Sunday I tried to convey the love of God that I have experienced, love that has finally nearly delivered me from the torment of obsessive compulsive disorder that had me damned for hell from one minute to the next, love that meets me and is waiting for me each morning when I show up, love that wants to tell me the secrets and mysteries of God, One that promises that he will protect me from my enemies and keep me safe and secure in his womb, One who will carry my anxieties of the day, and One who will never leave me or forsake me, One who finds the kind of joy in holding me that this grandfather finds in holding his grandson Ezra after three months of social isolation. Holding Ezra this past Sunday brought the kind of joy that few other things do. And to think that is just a fraction of what God experiences when we show up to be with him. I suspect his response is something like, "Ah, indeed, I thought you would call me father," as he grins from ear to ear.

The thing is, folks, this reality is not far from any of us—it is present among us. But too often we are not present to the One who makes the things of heaven deeply personal to us and for us. We have so many reasons for not developing a life with God—sitting with God, talking to God, being quiet and still before God, allowing God's eternal Word to enter our mortal pores.

Following the message on Sunday, we had an intergenerational class to discuss the sermon, as we have been doing since disassembling. As I listened to the conversation, it felt as if I were listening to a discussion about a different message. The points of the conversation we had were very good, but there was little discussion of the significance of experiencing the love of God or how one steps into that all-encompassing love, or what difference that love makes in our lives. I found myself grieving that afternoon.

But I understand; I have been there. I'm sure Walter grieved some of the messages he heard me preach when he often said, "That was a good word, BUT . . . " Because there was something I just wasn't getting according to Walter, and in retrospect I have to say Walter was right. You can't preach what you've not experienced, and you can't experience the love of God without a life with God that is surrendered to God.

Looking back, I felt like watching Walter somedays was like watching a freak show at the circus, with him jumping up unannounced, grinning from ear to ear, and throwing his arm from one side of his body to the other. But maybe that's exactly what it means to get in touch with God's love: It sends us over the edge into the depths and breadth and height and depth of that love, from which we cry out, "Please jump in—the water is just fine in here!"

The journey to the deep end is not complicated, folks. It begins and ends with "being still and knowing that [he is] God."

CHAPTER 26

Preacher Amanda Gorman
February 2021

I recently suggested that the help we need as a Church can only come from those who have experienced oppression and trauma, because these folks have learned how to create beauty, to sing and dance in the midst of the darkness and chaos and evil. Those of us in the center don't have much of a clue obviously, since we are the ones who got the Church into the mess it's in in the first place. We've done a great job of steering her directly into the rocks.

Poet Amanda Gorman only confirmed my suggestion with her incredibly God-inspired sermon/poem on the steps of the Capitol building where only two weeks earlier representatives of Christ's Church joined white supremacists in an insurrection that had nothing to do with heaven coming to earth, but rather hell itself. But on that Thursday, Amanda brought heaven back down with so many lines that invoked heaven's dream for the world including: "...If we merge mercy with might, and might with right, then love becomes our legacy, and change our children's birthright. So let us leave behind a country better than the one we were left with." Amen, Amanda, amen.

A church leader who listens to the podcast recently sent this note to me:

> I was listening lately to some of your podcasts "A Church Dismantled—A Kingdom Restored." I find these episodes very engaging and inspiring. Like you, I have a keen sense that the

Lord is challenging us to see the new thing he is doing and going back to the status quo would be a mistake. As our foundations continue to be shaken in recent years and particularly also in recent weeks, I sense the Lord saying, "You (the Church) got another chance to right the ship. There is only a small window for that to happen, though. Are you up for the task?" As you know, church multiplication is always on my heart but as you said in one of you your recent podcasts it matters what we multiply. Not everything is worth multiplying. I know that what we are building needs to be on the foundation of Jesus Christ. It must not be tainted with a quest for power or recognition. It will be costly and yet the results will be very beautiful. As I am thinking about these things, I have more questions than answers. I don't know what is worth keeping and what the new wine skins should look like? I don't know how Church should interact with culture and when are we just a light on the hill as an alternative community? How do we make disciples, that are actually recognizable followers of *the way*? Thanks for your willingness to tackle the hard questions, which I am sure does not always give you favor with the status quo Church. I'll keep listening with you to the Lord of the church for answers. Pray for me that he finds an obedient heart.

I responded with: "Friend, thank you for your kind and generous reflections and your understanding of my heart. I feel increasingly content to let the ship sink and to flee for rescue to the One who beckons us all home. The ship is incapable of saving itself, and I'm not confident it has the will or the desire to beckon its Lord or to even recognize that it is sinking. As I have become more converted to Jesus this year I feel further and further away from the Church we've created and more drawn to simply engage the world with the Good News and see what happens. I find that the Good News is still attractive even when the church has lost its savor."

Interestingly, one night this week I woke at 3:00 a.m. with the seafaring song "Haven of Rest" running through my head, a song that I have not listened to or sung for years: "My soul in sad exile was out on life's sea, So burdened with sin and distressed, Till I heard a sweet voice, Saying, 'Make Me your choice'; And I entered the 'Haven of Rest'! I've anchored my soul in the "Haven of Rest," I'll sail the wide seas no more; The tempest may sweep over wild, stormy, deep, In Jesus I'm safe evermore."

Oh, that the Church would begin to sing this song once again. But until it does, I, along with many of you, will do so.

Early in my writing this past year, I discussed the tension I feel in being at the intersection of the Church and the academy for the past thirty years. Typically that tension has come from being a follower of Jesus in a secular, academic setting. But over the past several years the greatest tension for me now lies in trying to follow Christ in a church that feels like it has become more and more reflective of violence and oppression and hostility of the world.

For indeed, together we are up to the grand excavation work of Isaiah 40—lowering mountains, raising valleys, making rough places plain and crooked places straight so that the glorious and loving and compassionate nature of who God is can be revealed to all humankind! This is our work together as a community. We may be on the margins of the Church, but we know that it is from the margins that the kingdom will arise and is already in much evidence. Just listen to Amanda Gorman's poem.

PART SIX

PASTORS AND SOUL CARE

CHAPTER 27

A Spiritual Director Speaks
to Pandemic Pastors
November 2020

Some time ago I interviewed Eldon Fry, my long-time spiritual director who has been a gift from God to me. After a difficult congregational conflict in which I experienced deep pain, followed by a fall from our roof and a broken hip in 2013, I finally reached out to Eldon for help. What help he has given to me over these years! I was struck by several really important points that he made during our interview that I think both pastors and congregations need to hear.

First, pastors don't know these days if their members are following them. As Eldon said, the feedback loop has been broken, and we hear very little from our members as to how we are leading except from those whose critical voices are not diminished by a little thing like a pandemic. Sociological theories about social roles tell us that our roles are always social and depend on not only playing the role of pastor but also having members who play their roles as well. When it is not clear that members are following, it is also not clear that as pastors we are still leading. This has a profound impact upon our sense of identity and our purpose.

Second, as rational, modern churches and church organizations, we have created metrics of success that are rational and can be counted, such as membership, attendance, baptisms, and budgets. Now, those metrics are largely meaningless, and it is increasingly clear that as leaders and congregations we have been putting our confidence in the wrong things. We've been counting things that are measurable but that don't matter. It's so much easier to count whether Raymond and Bertha are there on Sunday than whether Raymond and Bertha have a life with God or a life with the devil. And if it is the latter, what pastor in their right mind will approach them about that? Some of us have tried that and, well, paid a price that is quite measurable in the short-term. Perhaps it is time, however, to begin worrying about people's lives with God, regardless of whether or not they kick us out of the Church.

Third, pastors are more isolated than ever. Leadership is always done alone, but now we are more alone than ever before. As any pastor knows, having friends while in leadership is always a tenuous business, because at any moment we may say or do something that any of those friends might not appreciate, and given the attachment of God to everything in the Church, any of us can quickly take our case up a notch by claiming that the Almighty is really on our side. And so you end up with dueling saints, both convinced that heaven has come to earth through them, and when that happens, God help us. I've always found that congregational conflicts are much more heated and intense and endure longer than at the college where I teach. One person recently noted to me that they were sorry that I took so much heat at the Church and at the college, and I wanted to say, "But you have no idea—academia has always been a safer place for me to be than the Church."

Finally, as I have said for decades, the only solution to any of our problems now or ever has been the development of our life with God. And Eldon made that clear to me. I loved his example of the leader who said that nothing about my life with God will change in terms of my spiritual practices, because I've had in place what I needed to prepare me for that time.

Again, this is what I tell our congregation. I don't practice a life with God so that I can check that off my list or to help me just through this day. I have a life with God now in order to prepare me for the day of my death and the days of crisis between now and then. A life built with God now prepares me to meet God then. What I have learned over time as a pastor is that sometimes those who are the most critical of my leadership are also those whom I know have nurtured very little life with God. Because I have learned that behind every saint is always a life with God, and behind every life with God you will always find a saint. And behind every chronically discontent member is that absence of a life with God. And behind every discontented member is someone without a deep life with God.

So take courage, leaders. You will one day stand before God, and that critical saint will be nowhere around then. In fact, they may just be standing before God complaining about you and blaming you for why they weren't prepared for that day. But don't worry: Their arguments will stand about as much chance before God as President Trump's complaints about election fraud. If there is not fraud, then complaints on Twitter don't matter. And if there isn't any life with God, the complaints about you won't really matter on the day when what matters most is tested by fire.

So take heart, my pastor friend, and just sit down and hear that God does not shame you or condemn you but rather calls you his beloved son or daughter. There is good reason for Jesus to state that prophets are not accepted in their hometowns. Our hometown is so very, very temporary. We belong among those who are constantly restless for that city whose builder and maker is God, a city that perhaps pastors (in these days more than anyone) can't wait to see coming down!

CHAPTER 28

Birding With Eric—Hearing God's Voice or Just Watching From the Windows?
June 2020

Last Saturday, Heidi and I spent time with her cousin Eric Willet. He is a professional nature photographer whose astounding photos of wildlife in their own habitat can be found on his Facebook page. This was our second time to the Wildwood Nature Preserve near Harrisburg, Pennsylvania, and I was more impressed than ever by the difference between someone whose life has been given to studying and appreciating nature versus those of us who enjoy the scenery but spend little time inside it. I love observing people who are good at their craft, passionate about it, and willing to share with those of us who are not. For many of us, viewing nature is a hobby, a pastime in which we see creation behind the windows of our cars or our homes and we say, "What a sunset," or, "Wow, did you see that beautiful bird!" And then we go back to our lives.

Heidi and I love to watch the birds in our backyard, and we feed them the best mixes of fruits and nuts, worms and bugs, and suet. This year in particular we have enjoyed hosting warblers, a scarlet tanager, and an indigo bunting—all species we never saw at our feeders before. We were most drawn by the bluebird couple who consistently dive-bombed us when we got near their box, which at first contained eggs, and then hatchlings, and eventually a family of four siblings that fledged and also came to our feeder.

But being with Eric on Saturday was a different experience

altogether, because rather than drawing the birds to him by feeding them rich treats, he went out to them, as he does weekend after weekend at Wildwood, waiting for hours sometimes to get a photo of an egret feeding its young, a black snake eating a juvenile muskrat, a bald eagle swooping down for its breakfast, and so much more. Eric's photos are full of the movement of nature, nature that he sees only because he spends so much time inside it.

When we pulled into the park, for example, Eric pointed out a Baltimore oriole couple feeding their young high up in a tree. How he ever saw that nest was beyond me. He then asked, "Where are your binoculars?" We looked at each other like, "*Hello*, we are going birding this morning!"

Eric generously ran to his car to retrieve a set for us. Meanwhile, we were still trying to see the oriole nest! As we walked through the park, Eric would stop from time to time and say, "Listen, that's a wood thrush," or some other bird. In the midst of what sounded to me like a chorus of indistinguishable sounds, Eric could pick out one species after another. And when he heard where they were, he was able to see them more easily.

At one point we saw a black-capped night heron—a bird we'd never seen before and one he was anxious for us to see. "Look," Eric said, "it will place its beak in the algae, stir things up to attract a fish that thinks the movement means something to eat, and then it will grab the fish." Within about three minutes, what Eric described is exactly what happened. "Wow," he said, "I've stood here for hours waiting, just to see what you did in only a few minutes!" It was a lucky day for novices!

As we walked back to the car, I commented on his ability to see so much that we could not. He modestly said, "Well, I am here a lot—I know this place." And he is—every season of the year and in each season learning more about what can be seen when, and how the lowering lake level is affecting what can be seen and not seen.

Eric also noted that he uses his ears more than his eyes—that he is listening even more than watching. I thought about how open Eric's senses are to nature when he steps on the grounds of Wildwood, how tuned in he is to what is going on around him, and how fully present he must be in order to hear and see. And that it is in hearing first that he sees second.

I thought about God and our life with God, or our lack thereof. How seeing the movement of God's Spirit from tree to tree as it were, can't happen unless we are listening attentively to the voice of that Spirit, and can't happen if we are unable to distinguish the Spirit's voice from the chorus of other voices calling out to us. We can't even begin to see or hear the Spirit if we aren't practiced at doing so, if we've not spent hours waiting for a glimpse of the Spirit's movement and direction, and if we don't spend time in the habitat where the Spirit hangs out.

I sometimes hear folks say, "I've never heard God speak." My internal response these days is, "Stop, listen, and look." You can't hear God if you don't slow down long enough to do so, if you don't know the habitat where the Spirit hangs out, if you don't empty yourself to be present to the Spirit.

No, I believe that God is constantly speaking, and I believe that the skills of hearing his voice can indeed be honed. But none of that happens without spending time with God on a regular basis, without being present to God, sitting with God, waiting for God. God speaks to each of us in just the exact way that we can uniquely hear him, and after doing so one or two times, we begin to know that familiar voice among all the others. The sweetest of all voices it is, the kindest and most caring of all, the most generous and gracious of all.

I was also reminded in our time with Eric that most of us need a spiritual guide to get us started in this listening journey; we need someone like Eric who knows the habitat of God, who has listened and heard God, and who can point God out to us.

I sometimes hear folks say, "I don't need a spiritual guide or director. I don't know why that is necessary." Here is an exercise that will teach you quickly: Go out to Wildwood and walk for three hours and record what you hear and see. Then call Eric or one of his friends and ask them to walk with you for a few hours, and the answer will smack you in the face.

CHAPTER 29

Cornwall, Nouwen, and a Spirit Who Publicly Wounds the Healer
May 2021

Perhaps part of the reason that as a kid I was so taken by Judson Cornwall's little book *Freeway Under Construction* was the fact that here was a church leader who so openly described his undoing by the Spirit and who so freely embraced the public brokenness that he experienced in the midst of leading. Growing up in a culture where such brokenness was a sign of weakness or ungodliness, I suspect I found comfort in Cornwall's experience. For I was a kid who was so aware that I was different: mouthing prayers of forgiveness while hanging out with friends, pointing to the sky to try to get my prayers right, and writing prayers of forgiveness on the side of my blue book exams while other students were, well, taking their exams, and on and on. All the while trying to find peace with a God who everyone said was Love.

My experiences of pain and brokenness have mostly been public things: from a broken marriage in a valley where good people always had happy marriages, to two bouts of cancer, and now tremors that tell everyone that I'm anxious and that what's on the inside is seen on the outside. There's been no hiding the Spirit's dismantling in my life.

And so I identified with Cornwall so fully when he noted that we love when, "the Spirit flows like a placid river . . . within our lives," but, "feel we could do well without His explosive ministry. We want to be built up, not torn down . . . . Must these ministries, gifts, and graces of God be reduced to rubble just so that God can build a road? Yes!"[33]

He goes on to describe the, "inner terror, the feeling of insecurity, and the sense of unfairness when God began to strip down my high ridges of the operation of the gifts of the Spirit through me and began to manifest them through the members of the congregation."[34] He describes a breakdown in the pulpit one Sunday morning that left him in tears, an experience that lasted three weeks. During this time, it was the members of the congregation that stepped in and began to minister.

Said Cornwall:

> My highest ministries were being exploded into rubble, but a roadway was being built right into the presence of God. My "heights" of ability and strength of ministry had become an insurmountable barrier to their getting to God. So God reduced me to tears while bringing them through to His presence. Let the high places go. Of course those exalted ridges must come down! Those doctrinal highs, those experiential highs, those emotional elevations must be lowered to get a road through the wilderness . . . . Even though we may have developed the strength and consistency of a rock, if it is in the way of the road to God's glory it will have to be blasted out . . . . So God allows the Spirit to reduce our great strength to gravel.[35]

Here was a Christian, let alone a leader, who was acknowledging that much of the brokenness we experience is because the Spirit is using his dynamite to blow us up, and that we can and must let go

---

33   Judson Cornwall, *Freeway under Construction* (Bellingham: Logos, 1978), 23.
34   *Freeway Under Construction,* 23
35   *Freeway Under Construction,* 24-25.

of our efforts to try holding both the Church and our own personal enterprise together.

Which brings me to Henri Nouwen's thesis of the "wounded healer" and my long struggle with what I understood Nouwen to be saying: that as a leader it is important to reveal our weakness as a sort of object lesson for others whom we are leading, while not completely letting slip what a mess we truly are, lest they sense the need to care for us and we become dependent on them for support. Which is all well and good if one can conceal one's brokenness and if one can keep the lid on the Spirit's dynamite. But what happens when the Spirit takes over? And what happens when one's weaknesses can't be concealed? What happens when in dismantling the Church, the Spirit must begin by dismantling its leaders?[36]

I get enough implicit hints and explicit overtures these days to know that some are concerned that over the past year some of my high places have been laid to waste. Some wonder what happened to the person I used to be. My answer continues to be, though perhaps unsatisfying to some and even heretical to others, that I've had an experience with the Spirit who has blown a lot of me up. Who I was too often was a barrier to others experiencing God's glory rather than part of that Isaiah 40 highway.

To fulfill my dream of joining in that grand excavation project that I dreamt of as a kid reading Judson Cornwall down in the woods below our house, I had to be excavated first. And when the Spirit blows up so much of what we took for granted to be true, we just might speak in tongues that are troubling, if not unintelligible, to those still living in that former reality. But given the contentment and peace and love I've found with God these days, I'm okay with that.

---

[36]   Henri Nouwen, *The Wounded Healer* (Baltimore, MD: Image, 1979).

CHAPTER 30

Those Who Refuse the Bread
Are So Easy to Spot
March 2021

I 've been listening in the morning to the hymn "Abide with Me." This song was written during the Civil War by Martin Lowrie Hofford, a period in U.S. history that many suggest as a parallel to the division and polarization of our current context. The first verse goes like this:

> Abide with me, fast falls the eventide. The darkness deepens, Lord, with me abide. When other helpers fail and comforts flee, Help of the helpless, oh, abide with me.[37]

Perhaps the central theme of my preaching over the past decade has been just this: "Nurture your life with God. Come to know him. Come to know his deep love for you. Just as we need to eat and drink, so we need to feed upon the One who is the Bread of Life." I have repeatedly said that if we do not develop a life with God, we will have no foundation to stand upon when trouble comes. There is only so much that others can do for us in such moments. "When other helpers fail and comforts flee," we are left with the reality of just how thin our life with God has been.

In John 6, Jesus tells those around him that he is the bread come down from God:

---

[37]   https://www.hymnal.net/en/hymn/h/370.

"I am the bread of life. Whoever comes to me will never be hungry, and whoever believes in me will never be thirsty. But I said to you that you have seen me and yet do not believe. Everything that the Father gives me will come to me, and anyone who comes to me I will never drive away; for I have come down from heaven, not to do my own will, but the will of him who sent me (John 6:35–38).

Predictably, those around Jesus again began to grumble at his words, reminding each other that he was no one other than Joseph and Mary's son, and so it was highly improbable that he could really be bread from heaven. One of my greatest griefs as I transition out of ministry is the recognition that while some have heard and responded, evidenced by the peace they express and the stillness one sees in their lives, it is also so clear that others have not done so. How can one tell those who have regularly eaten of the Bread of Life from those who have not? The same way that Jesus could tell: the grumbling gives it away.

It's hard to be a chronic grumbler when you are abiding with Christ. It's difficult to remain bitter and angry when your hands are open to receive the bread from heaven. But grumblers inevitably close their hands in a fist, and closed hands have a hard time receiving anything, let alone the Bread of Life. A steady diet of that Bread brings healing, touches us where we most need to be touched, resolves the answers that others cannot give us, and meets the deep hunger in our souls. It is from this place of fulfillment and nourishment that we greet the world and that we greet one another.

Whether we greet the world grumbling or greet the world with grace has everything to do with whether we have practiced abiding with the only One who can satisfy our weary souls. As our congregation regathers, I will be listening for the grumbling. It will tell me and everyone else who spent this past year abiding and who did not, who spent this last year feeding on the Bread from heaven and who did not.

PART SEVEN

PASTORS
AND PREACHING

The Kids of Disgruntled Saints and a Dismantled Church—the Secrets I Keep With Them and What I've Never Told Their Parents

July 2020

O ver the last three decades I have had the gift of relating to eighteen to twenty-two year olds, who first saw me as a peer and now see me as a grandfather. Regardless of how they see me, they have given me the gift of their trust. Some of them are Evangelicals, many are Roman Catholic, some are from the mainline Protestant churches, some are Muslim, Hindu, Wiccan, not associated with any religious tradition, or are agnostic or atheists.

But what they have shared with me are their hearts and their secrets. Some of them are actually children of members of my congregation, and while most are not, they have still represented their cohorts from Millennials to Generation X, Y, and now Z. Why we have given them such ridiculous labels is beyond me, but perhaps it's better than my cohort, which is called the "Young Boomers." I mean, how long are we going to defy the reality that if you were born between 1955 and 1964, you are hardly a young boomer or young *anything* anymore?

In any event, I have for decades felt the tension of hearing the secrets of my students in the classroom and how to address these concerns in sermons that I preach. I shared my dilemma and the tension I feel with a group of parents from our congregation a few weeks ago during a Zoom call following a sermon. To their great credit, they asked me to please preach to their children rather than to them—to preach what their children needed to hear rather than what they as parents necessarily wanted to hear.

One of the special things about being a pastor is that people write you emails and texts and letters. Some of these are less than encouraging and take me a few days or weeks to release to the Lord. But one of the consistent and intriguing things to me over the years is that among the saints who are most disgruntled about what I preach and teach and are willing to let me know, are their children, who then send me supportive and affirming and encouraging notes and emails that are 180 degrees opposite of the tone and the language of their parents.

In other words, while I've heard secrets in the classroom, I also get them by email from eighteen to thirty-year olds, for whom I am so grateful, because I am no longer preaching so much to their parents as to them, and their communication with me allows me to know whether they are hearing me or not.

Over the years I also have had the privilege of meeting for breakfast, lunch, and coffee with many of the young adults from our congregation, whose trust I have apparently earned as they have grown up with me as their primary pastor. One called me early one morning, about 4:00 a.m., somewhat hungover, asking if I would come visit so that they could share a secret with me they needed to get off their chest. Another approached me with money, saying, "Please put this in the offering—it's to take care of something I did some time ago." Another sent me a prophetic word of blessing and affirmation of the joy that God finds in me and that God trusts me, just around the time I was hearing the very opposite from her parents.

Noah ben Shea tells the story of parents who are walking down a path in front of their children. The children cannot see around the parents—they only see the parent's coattails. So they ask the parents what's ahead, and the parents can't explain to them why they are going on the path they are going on. They have just always done it. In turn, the children turn away from their parents because they are looking for honesty, for something true to believe in, for guides who have walked the way before them and can at least tell them why they are going the way they are going.[38]

That's about where we are with the Church these days. Too many parents who've forgotten why we are on this path anyway and who have lost the language to share this with their children. And so the children are bailing out of the Church at a higher rate than ever before. But when you don't know why you are on the path in the first place, there isn't much you can do to keep your children on that path.

Christian Smith, an Evangelical sociologist of religion from Notre Dame, in describing the drift from faith of Evangelical youth, pins the blame solidly on their parents. The kids didn't just get this way—they were *made* this way, formed in a society where the voice of the Church has diminished to taking up only one or two hours a week, and within homes where parents are trying to keep up with the American dream more than anything else and count it success if their children are better off in social status than they were, and in a world where social media is the loudest voice our kids hear (and, of course, it is not one voice—it is a million voices).[39]

So who can blame our kids for being lost? Their parents were lost a long time ago.

What are the secrets I hear?

"I don't endorse Donald Trump, but my parents do, and I have to get out of the house—I can't take it anymore." Parents, when you

---

[38]   Noah ben Shea, *Jacob the Baker* (New York: Ballantine Books, 1990).

[39]   Christian Smith and Patricia Snell, *Souls in Transition* (New York: Oxford, 2009).

tie Jesus to Donald Trump and suggest through word and deed that to be a follower of Jesus is to follow Donald Trump, then you are setting your children up to leave Jesus. Because you have tied the two so closely together, your kids are literally believing that to have Jesus is to have Trump. Would you rather your children go to heaven as Democrats, or to hell by embracing a particular president or politician but having rejected Jesus?

"I am gay and I can't tell anybody else about it. It is terrible walking into church and knowing that if I shared this one thing, I would be rejected, even though I am still the same person that people accept right now." Folks, I don't pretend to have an easy answer. I know we have to find a way to create space for our children to discuss everything they are struggling with. They need to know we love them no matter what secrets they tell us. I am convinced that if Jesus is in the midst of these conversations, we will find our way through them.

"I believe in science, global warming, and the coronavirus." What strikes me most about this one is that our kids are growing up in an entirely rational age that we as parents have embraced. We encourage them to go to college and to follow their dreams and hearts and callings. But then when they go to college and encounter rationality and science, we tell them not to believe what they are learning and that if they do believe this stuff, then they don't believe the Bible. But, folks, the Christian life is about believing in Jesus and loving Jesus and having a relationship with Jesus—not about whether our kids believe that God used evolution in the creation process (which is something I do endorse and learned at my own Evangelical alma matter, Wheaton college) or whether they believe the coronavirus is real and whether climate change is occurring. One young person told me that their parents said that if they didn't believe in the literal creation story, then they didn't believe the rest of the Bible either. Again, would we rather this child go to heaven embracing an evolution narrative, or to hell having thrown out the Bible with the bathwater?

"I drink alcohol and don't understand what the problem is." To be honest with you, young person, many of your parents drink also, even if they do it when you aren't looking. Folks, our kids are not into prohibition or into temperance and the reasons we are giving them that they should be aren't making biblical sense to them. So let's be honest and transparent and teach them about the risks of substance use and abuse and the health concerns that too much alcohol consumption can create. *That* they will connect with.

Finally I hear this: "My parents taught me that only Christians are happy and good and find life meaningful, but when I went to university and college I found lots of friends who seemed to be making it just fine, and so I'm not sure that following Jesus is the only way." Again, parents, if we make being a Christian about being happy and finding meaning and being good, then we are creating the foundation of what Christian Smith calls the "moralist therapeutic deistic" Christianity that our children are embracing.

No, the Christian faith is so much more cosmic and on a grander scale than my meaning and happiness and goodness—it is the invitation to join God in his grand excavation project of Isaiah 40, of lowering mountains that keep people oppressed and from joining God's highway, of raising the valleys where the oppressed and marginalized have been forced to reside, or making rough places plain and crooked places straight. God has a place for each of us on that project. That is way bigger than whether I am good or happy or finding meaning in my life.

That is why I am on the path I am on, for this is the good news God has for all of creation: There is a new kingdom coming where lion and lamb will lie down together forever.

CHAPTER 32

From "Don't Preach to Me" to Coffee with Bruno at Turkey Hill to "Where'd That Preacher Go?" and . . . Does One Need to Be "Preachy in Order to Preach?"

October 2020

I would always have described Murray as a bit crusty around the edges. In our first season of ministry, perhaps more than once when I attempted to invite him to church he would turn and growl, "Don't preach to me." I soon learned to be cautious when I saw Murray. His wife attended our congregation regularly and had prayed for decades for her husband.

Over the last several years, I would run into Murray in the mornings at our local convenience store, outside with his beautiful yellow lab, Bruno. I would periodically buy Murray a coffee and say a few words to Bruno. Murray always had something to say and then he would let out a kind of cynical laugh. I knew better than to preach to Murray. But I could buy him coffee and say hi to Bruno. Maybe that was the best preaching I could do.

We had known for some time that Murray was having back trouble. Heidi placed him on our prayer list and stayed in touch with his wife. But less than two weeks ago it was discovered that Murray's pain was due to stage 4 lung cancer, and the doctors gave him six months or less to live. When I heard this news, I sensed God telling me that I had no choice but to visit Murray. So Heidi spoke with Shirley and asked if Murray would allow us to visit. Shirley replied that Murray had already asked that I come over to the house. So five days after his diagnosis, Heidi and I visited Murray in his home. He welcomed us warmly, even as he quipped, "Now don't be preaching to me."

I realize now that what Murray had associated with preaching was clearly not good news. Whatever preaching had been for Murray, it obviously had not been comforting to him. Whatever preaching was for Murray, it was something to defend and protect himself from—which is just an incredible shame—something that Murray likely felt when he heard such preaching. Somewhere along the way, Murray felt the need to defend himself from what should have been good news.

Which brings me back to a constant theme of mine over the past fifteen years: that the Church is being dismantled precisely because it has done so much to make the good news bad news. It has made preaching more about sending people to hell than calling them into heaven; it has made preaching more about shame than about grace, more about damnation than salvation. I don't blame Murray for telling me not to preach at him—ever since the revivals I experienced when I was a kid in Big Valley, Pennsylvania, I haven't liked to be preached at either.

In a related question, Mike the bike guy, my Jewish, agnostic, sociologist friend, asked me a couple of weeks ago, "Is it possible to preach without being preachy? You know what I mean," he said. I had to agree that I did. For the only times Jesus got preachy was when he was with the Pharisees, who were the last to think they needed Jesus's preaching. But Jesus didn't get preachy among those whom most of us think need the preaching the most. The last thing he did was preach at them.

Mike said he didn't think I was preachy, and I was glad to hear that. I suspect if I were preachy, Mike wouldn't have lasted as one of my best friends. Because the last thing Mike himself is is preachy. Instead, he listens, observes, tells stories, and in doing so over the decades has impacted me more than anyone else in terms of applying the sociological perspective to the world around me. Though Mike does not claim any religious identity or faith commitment, he practices the best of what good preaching is: listening, observing, and then telling stories that connect with what people most need to hear about the good news. Some days that's a cup of coffee at Turkey Hill.

In any event, as Heidi and I met with Murray, I asked him if he was ready to meet God. "I don't know," he said. So I asked if we could pray. He agreed, and at his request we all held hands as Murray made his peace with God. Heidi gave him a small cross to hold, and he has clung to that cross ever since, as if his life depends on it; for of course, his, like all of ours, does.

Shirley later told Heidi that when Murray didn't know they were watching, they would see him clutching the cross and praying. He also called his family to gather around him and to hold the cross together and to pray. And when they said, "Amen," Murray was heard joining them.

As I visited yesterday with this newly reborn saint, I read Psalm 23 and prayed with him. The family gathered around. Thinking he was sleeping again, I took my hand from his arm and moved away from the bed. Suddenly we heard, "Where is that preacher at?" And so I went back and drew up a chair and read John 14 and suggested we all sing "Amazing Grace." As we did so, Murray's lips formed the words with us: "Amazing grace, how sweet the sound, that saved a wretch like me, I once was lost but now am found, was blind but now I see."

Before leaving, again thinking my friend was asleep, I chuckled as I shared with the family that their husband and father had gone from telling me not to preach to him to asking, "Where is that preacher?" We looked at Murray, and he had a big smile on his face.

Yes, in the end all things are dismantled on this earth. But this world is not our home, and we are only passing through. On the other side awaits beauty and peace and all things good, where we will finally be home free. As I told my friend yesterday, you are now on the safest trip you could ever be on; you are safer now than ever before. The step from here to there is only a small one, and the One who holds your hand now will hold it the whole way home.

The next day I got word that Murray had indeed gone home.

CHAPTER 33

Perilous Preaching in an Age of Pandemic, Protests, and Polarization
September 2020

T he lines between podcasting and preaching are blurring for me as I become more honest in all the places God has called me to, about who I am and what exactly is my story and my song. As I do so, I find that I am much less anxious at Elizabethtown College about speaking the truth of my life with God and its implications for my view of the world, than I am in the Church these days doing the same. This is not a critique of my own congregation, but an awareness that my understanding of what it means to be a follower of Jesus in the midst of this pandemic, the political polarization that divides us, and the fires of efforts to bring racial reconciliation and justice do not line up with what so many others believe in the broader Church. And so yesterday, as always these days, when I tremor on the inside, it becomes clear on the outside.

I shared with the congregation that I have largely focused on the nurturing of our life with God over my years of preaching—and this is true. I believe that all we do and say and how we live flows out of the degree to which we have a life with God and have an intimate connection to him. I also believe that any concerns we have about justice in the world must flow from that life with God, or we will eventually tire of the fight, lose heart, and abandon the cross. It is as we live life with the Author and Perfecter of our faith that we endure the cross and keep in sight the "joy set before us."

But when I look at the Church these days, what I see is that either we have no life with God, or we have such a thin life with God that it makes no difference in our ethic or how we live our lives, or we simply don't see the connection between life with God and the life to be lived in the world that God so loved and so loves still.

I preached from Ephesians 2 and 3, where the apostle Paul declares that Christ has come to dismantle the dividing wall between Jew and Gentile, that the two are now one body in Christ Jesus. That Christ is our peace in making the two who were hostile toward one another one through the cross. This, says Paul, is the mystery of Christ. The mystery of Christ is that his death and resurrection destroyed not only barriers between God and humankind but also barriers between humankind and humankind.

The division and barrier between white and Black in this country began with the forced enslavement of West African men, women, and children—who were forced at gunpoint onto ships to endure conditions that none of us today would even consider to be acceptable for livestock. But that was the point: These human beings from the beginning were seen as nothing besides property, property to be used for economic gain by white Europeans in the New World's plantations, plantations owned and operated by the founders of this nation. Thousands upon thousands of these men, women, and children died during their transport across the Atlantic, and when they arrived upon the shores of the "land of the free and home of the brave," they had already been stripped of their human dignity and freedom. If anyone were brave, it was certainly they. And yet, like our Lord, both at his birth and during his ministry, they found no home when they got here.

The word "race" doesn't show up in the English language until the time of the slave trade, and its emergence is directly tied to being a Black slave. Thinking of oneself as white was a new thing also up to that point, but suddenly the color of one's skin, or what E.B. Dubois calls "the color line," became written into the fabric of this nation. The sin of declaring one group of God's children as less than human and treating them as such for the last four hundred years is sin that this country is paying for now and will continue to do so for decades to come. As African American Bishop Al Motley once told me, "the work of anti-racism" is spiritual warfare. If we who are white had experienced the enslavement, lynchings, family separations, rape, assaults and beatings, separate but not equal facilities, police brutality, and mass incarceration of Black men—we too would have no trouble seeing the demonic in this history.

Stepping into the message yesterday, I was tremoring extraordinarily, aware that I was stepping into the middle of this war against the mystery of Christ that is being fought in the heavenlies. We who are pastors know that if it is safety and security we seek as preachers, and if that becomes our point of reference, we will never be part of lowering the mountains and raising the valleys of Isaiah 40, of making rough places plain and crooked places straight. No, every excavation project has huge risks to those who enter it—some will lose their lives there, as did Martin Luther King, Jr., who had an uncanny sense just before his assassination that he had gotten to the top of the mountain like Moses, but that he just might not get to enjoy the fruit of the uphill struggle that had gotten him there.

Pastors, the author of Ecclesiastes (9:12) warned us about this day: "Moreover, no one knows when their hour will come. As fish are caught in a cruel net, or birds are taken in a snare, so individuals are trapped by evil times that fall unexpectedly upon them" (NIV). Evil times that fall unexpectedly are upon us, pastors. If you are paying any attention at all, these times are here. Times not unlike what Martin Luther found himself within, times not unlike what Dietrich Bonhoeffer found himself in during the Third Reich, not unlike what Martin Luther King, Jr., John Lewis, Ralph Abernathy, and so many other saints throughout history have found themselves in.

As I was tremoring and preaching outside in our parking lot yesterday, suddenly the bells of a neighboring church began to peal to the tune of "A Mighty Fortress Is Our God." As the bells rang out, I found I could not compete with the sound, and so I just stopped, and we listened. In that moment I recalled my favorite stanza from that hymn, a stanza that reminds us that Luther knew the battle that he had been dropped into in his generation, but that he also knew that the One who had unexpectedly called him to that battle was more than sufficient to ensure that the Truth of God would overcome the Prince of Darkness with just one little word—that word above all earthly powers—the One made flesh, who came to a planet where all hell was breaking out then just as it is now.

"And though this world, with devils filled, Should threaten to undo us, We will not fear, for God hath willed His truth to triumph through us. The Prince of Darkness grim—We tremble not for him; His rage we can endure, For lo! His doom is sure—One little word shall fell him."[40]

That word who came not to fell the political powers of that world or to conquer that world or to raise up an army against the Roman Empire, but to sneak quietly and unnoticed into that world, ambushing and overthrowing those powers by a greater power—the power of love—not of rage, division, or confusion—such inferior powers that in the end of time will along with the devil himself be thrown back where they came from.

But the love that casts out all fear? Keep preaching it, fellow pastor—that's how the story ends.

---

[40]   https://hymnary.org/text/a_mighty_fortress_is_our_god_a_bulwark.

CHAPTER 34

For Pastors Preparing to Preach in That Perilous Pulpit Once Again Tomorrow

September 2020

P reaching during this season of a pandemic, protests on behalf of racial justice, and political polarization that threaten to upend the presidential election, is difficult and potentially dangerous for the one who gets behind the pulpit each week. The division within the country has found its way into our churches such that there is often little tolerance for pastors to address the very issues that are right smack in front of us in the news every day. Politics has become the new sacred cow for the Church. Pastors are given space to preach as long as what they preach doesn't smell of being political. But what sounds like the gospel to one may sound like politics to another. The problem is that we live in a culture in which everything has been politicized, so that the trick of the devil is that if a pastor is to satisfy those in the pew, the list of things they can preach about is increasingly limited. For even God and the Bible have been politicized, and when that happens, there really isn't anything a pastor can safely get away with except perhaps greeting the saints·with a smile and having an opening prayer, followed by a benediction.

But this scene isn't new to the Church, because the devil isn't very creative. It was faced by Paul in the first century just as the Church was getting off the ground. Paul talks about divisions between those who loved Paul, those who loved Apollos, those who loved Peter, and, oh yes, those who loved Jesus. Paul is aware that a church with walls is an immature church, a church that has not yet lived into the mystery of Christ, which he preaches about in Ephesians 2 and 3. The mystery that there was One in the universe who could tear down the dividing wall of hostility between Jew and Gentile. I suspect, given Peter's difficulty overcoming this new mystery, that Paul's proclamations in Ephesians 2 and 3 sounded a bit like political propaganda to the Church fathers back in Jerusalem who raised their eyebrows as they read Paul's letter to the church at Ephesus. It makes me wonder if they wished they had had the power to censure Paul.

But, nope, Paul says in I Corinthians 4—ain't nobody except God going to be my judge. Paul was not going to get caught in the middle between those who saw the good news he proclaimed as gospel freedom and those who may have seen it as propaganda that they rejected for the teaching of Apollos. Paul was so incredibly focused on one thing—and that one thing was Christ crucified and that grand mystery was that in Christ every wall had to come down, between Jew and Gentile, male and female, slave and free. And if that sounded political to his audience, I get the sense from I Corinthians 4 that Paul could just about not care less. Just think for a minute how radical Paul's message of equality across these dividing walls had to sound to everyone who heard it. What sounded like politics and propaganda to those in power (Jews, men, and the masters of slaves) undoubtedly sounded like the bells of freedom to those on the margins (Gentiles, women, and slaves). Imagine what it must have sounded like to the Gentile, to the woman whose husband had abandoned her, and to the slave biding his time until he could run away into the night.

Because, you see, as I've mentioned before, who you are and where you sit in society's social hierarchy has a big impact on how you hear the gospel—as politics or as freedom! What we have done without being aware of it as a Church is to privatize our politics, to separate them out from the scrutiny of the Church and to argue that my politics are my business and not the Church's, and certainly not the pastor's. I get to make my own decisions about my political preferences, and the Church has no right to inform those decisions, unless the preacher happens to agree with my political preferences. I wonder what we just might tell Jesus to avoid teaching or preaching about today because it is just a tad too private and personal and we're not sure we want him telling us what we should do.

I have long told my students that in the modern world we have separated out our religious beliefs and commitments from the other areas of our lives—from our work, from our recreation, from our finances, from our sexual activities, from our education, from our political engagements, and on and on. Going to church and being a Christian is one thing we do and one part of who we are, but these do not dictate the rest of our disintegrated selves.

For those members who do not want their preacher to preach about issues related to politics, what are they ultimately saying? Are they saying that the Bible has no relevance to social and political issues? Are they saying that they know best personally about these things and don't need anyone else speaking into their lives about them, unless it's their favorite talk show host? Or are they saying, "Preacher, we also don't want you speaking about other private issues such as sexuality, we don't want you speaking to our finances because this is a private thing, we don't want you speaking about going to war, because I have my own personal views on this, we don't want you addressing the sacredness of marriage because we don't agree with you." Where does this kind of reasoning stop once we start down this road?

Which raises the question for all of us: Is there just a chance that in this time of global upheaval, national chaos, and many reasons to be anxious, we have decided to take things into our own hands—to give up on God's Word as the source of our faith and life and future, and to build a small golden calf that seems so much more relevant to us, or to find a ninety-foot statue to worship because the king we worship has told us to do so and all the other Christians seem to be doing it too?

Pastor, this is a time for courage. This is a time to reclaim the place of scripture for every area of our lives. This is a time to reclaim the ethic of Jesus, who came not only to bring us back to God through his death and resurrection, but who also spent three years teaching us how to live in a world that was falling apart then as much as our world is today. This is a time to stand with a long line of reformers who, in speaking God's truth regardless of the cost, are remembered for having salvaged the Church at a time when it otherwise might have been lost.

If you listen to what Jesus taught and how he lived his life, what you will see and hear is one who largely ignored the politics of his day and instead spent his time telling stories about the kingdom of God to the down and outers—a kingdom that as he said that was not of this world. Those stories often focused on why Jesus had come to be with us in the first place, "to preach good news to the poor, bind up the brokenhearted, proclaim freedom for the captives, and release from darkness for the prisoner." But, like today, that message sounded strikingly political to those in power, and for that political message our Lord found himself in deep trouble with those in power.

Pastor, tomorrow morning we are telling stories of a kingdom much greater than the one with the sacred cows, golden calves, and ninety-foot towers. We are telling stories about a kingdom that will put to dust those cows, calves, and towers one day. If telling such stories gets us into a fiery furnace or hauled off to the top of a hill somewhere, don't worry, we will be in good company either way. That fourth man is already there waiting for us, and his word to us will be, "Well done, good and faithful servant."

PART EIGHT

SOME FINAL WORDS
TO A CHURCH DISMANTLED

CHAPTER 35

We Asked for a King and God Gave Us a Shepherd
October 2020

When the people of God lived in the land of Canaan after the last of the judges had died, the scripture says that Israel had no king and every man did what was right in his own eyes. As Samuel the prophet declined in years, the people of God asked Samuel for a king like all the other nations had. Samuel was unhappy with the request, but God told him that it was God himself as their king they were rejecting and not Samuel. God instructed Samuel to give them their king but to warn them that they would live to regret their words.

So Samuel anointed a good-looking guy named Saul, who before too long would turn out to be just the kind of king God had warned the people they would regret. A king who rejected God. A king who God rejected. And so Samuel went looking for another king, but try as he might, he could not find a king among the sons of Jesse—not until that shepherd boy was called in from the fields, that shepherd boy who never thought (like most likely everyone else) that he would be Israel's next king.

But God had had it with kings who rejected him, and I suspect that what he wanted as much as anything else was a shepherd he could make into a king, who would receive on-the-job training as it were. But not just anyone could be trained to be the king that God knew his people needed. It's likely the last individual folks had in mind for the role would have been a shepherd who composed songs during long days sitting in the field in the sun alongside his sheep.

But God needed someone who was first and foremost a person after God's own heart, who already had an intimate life with God and who would lead from his life with God. Someone when he failed would be quick to say, "I am sorry"; who would be a man after God's own heart because he was contrite, soft, tender, broken, repentant; who would be a worshipper of God rather than a worshipper of the opinions of others.

And so God gave his people David, because (I like to think) he knew they needed a shepherd more than they needed a king, just as we still do. And yet, until the day of our death we so often yearn for a king and not a shepherd. But when it comes to our death, we almost always turn to Psalm 23. For on the day of our death, we need someone to walk us home, a shepherd who knows where to find us, a shepherd who knows where the sheep pen is, a shepherd who is guarding the sheep pen, a shepherd who has laid down his life for the sheep so that they can be part of his fold.

With Christ as our shepherd, we will be placed in a safe space—even when the mountains seem to be falling down around us; for with Christ our safety is not measured by whether we are sick or whether we get injured; the safety that Christ provides us is so much greater than that. It is the safety and security of our souls; of who we are at the center of ourselves; of who we are as people created in God's image. We can live within that safety regardless of whether we are dying or living. I told Murray, and I believe this, that for those who know Christ, the journey from this life to the next is no more than a simple step, and though we don't know exactly what the journey is like or what awaits us, it is the safest journey we have ever taken. Why? Because we are being led by the good Shepherd who has created a home for us and who knows the way back home.

Folks, the greatest danger we will face is not whether we get sick, not whether we get in an accident, not whether our country holds together, not whether riots break out around us. No, with Christ as our shepherd we can be safe regardless. The greatest danger that Murray Graham faced when he got the news of terminal cancer was not that he was dying, it was that he was dying without knowing for sure that he had a shepherd who would guide him home. The greatest question at the moment we walked into Murray and Shirley's home was not, "How long does Murray have?" but, "Is Murray at peace with his Shepherd or ready to make peace?" When Murray recognized that he needed God, everything else that he needed was going to be taken care of and paled in comparison to what he had received. And it was clear that Murray knew that.

Because Jesus is our shepherd, we can walk without fear through the shadows of death—shadows that sometimes whisper threats, shadows that sometimes move as if they will come back to haunt us, shadows that seem to be as alive as our memories of what the shadows represent. But they cannot harm us either, any more than death can, which for the follower of Jesus is also no more than a shadow. Compared to the glory that awaits us, compared to that home that is just a few steps away, death is only a shadow. Why? Because what death was meant to be when it emerged from the pit of hell on that awful day when we lost our innocence in the Garden of Eden, has been stripped away by the Good Shepherd who lay down his life for his sheep by entering into the fires of death. By doing so, for his flock death became only a shadow and not the real thing. For the one who turns to Christ, death has no victory and death has no sting—not for those who served Jesus for many decades and not for Murray who Jesus gave enough time to turn to him. For it is the will of the Shepherd that none, none, none, and no one should perish.

The Westminster Catechism asks "What is your only comfort in life and in death?" It then responds with the answer being "that I am not my own, but belong body and soul, both in life and in death, to my faithful Savior Jesus Christ."[41]

I recently heard two church leaders say two things that were simple but profound in the context of our world today and of we as a church. The first said, "I'm afraid our people have forgotten their homeland." In a different context, a second said, "We always want a king." What's interesting to me is that those who know they are dying have no trouble remembering their homeland and the last thing they call for is a king. No, their eyes are suddenly fixed on the eternal and their hearts now given to the only One who could get us from here to there. For when we suddenly get the word that we are dying, what was important now becomes not so much and what may have been not so important suddenly becomes the only thing we care about.

What would change within you and within us if we lived the rest of our days as if we were going to die? Because, of course, we are going to. Are you living with your true homeland in mind? This November, as we anticipate a tense election for President in the United States, are you crying out for a shepherd or a king?

---

[41]   http://www.heidelberg-catechism.com/en/lords-days/1.html.

CHAPTER 36

Dear Dismantled Church—Please Do Not Turn Back to the Managers
February 2020

The temptation for a people in the midst of disruption and chaos and confusion is always to look for stability and equilibrium. Émile Durkheim, the early French sociologist, made this case as he observed post-revolution France and the disruption it had experienced. Human beings fear anomie—that experience of losing sense of what is normative and the sense of deep aloneness that chaos can bring.

Thus, the tendency for God's people in the midst of a pandemic, economic uncertainty, and political polarization is to look for stability and solid ground wherever it might appear to be located. The problem is that this instinct just might be the wrong one to act upon in this moment of disruption brought on by God's Spirit. Just as the psalmist, in the midst of the mountains falling into the sea (chapter 46), counseled, "Be still and know that I am God," this may be our best choice now as well.

But it takes patience to be still. It takes faith to be still. And when we haven't practiced stillness before God in times of stability, it is unlikely that our instincts will be to turn to God in stillness when all hell seems to be breaking loose around us. No, in times of disruption, we too often turn to just about anything other than stillness before God. Instead, we call for a king like all of the other nations. Or we create a golden calf that at least we can see and touch. Or we turn back to the managers and away from the prophets and apostles—the latter being the ones who can both see in the midst of disruption and have been gifted to lead (and even sometimes create) disruption. But stillness, waiting, patience in an earthquake and in a pandemic and in a dismantled Church?

In his recent book *Tempered Resilience*, Tod Bolsinger describes the difference between managers and leaders. Managers are those who receive "a grateful response from those whom we manage." Managers take care of the assets of an organization and see stewarding those assets as their calling.[42]

Leaders on the other hand are "often met with stubborn resistance from the very people we are called to lead." Bolsinger notes that because we are wired for stability, we resist leaders and prefer managers. We just want things to run smoothly again. But in a moment when change is occurring, Bolsinger says that "we need leaders who can stand it when we resist the very thing we want and need, even to the point where we will turn on them, oppose them, sabotage them."[43]

In this moment, the Church in the U.S. is experiencing massive disruption and uncertainty. The temptation of congregations, mid-level judicatories, and denominations is to turn away from the apostolic and prophetic voices who are called and gifted precisely for such seasons, and to turn back to managers, administrators, and bureaucrats who promise stability and a return to the status quo. While these gifts are an important part of the Church, it is giving them the primary leadership over the past one hundred years that has gotten the Church into the mess it is in currently.

For with the onset of modernity, the Church quickly adapted the attributes and structures and values of professional, bureaucrat-

---

[42]   *Tempered Resilience*, 3
[43]   *Tempered Resilience*, 4

ic organizations with bylaws, complex flow charts, strategic plans, think tanks, buildings, and on and on. But these were precisely the things that Max Weber, a sociologist writing in Germany in the early 1900s, promised would trap the modern, rational world in an iron cage where it would experience, in language that feels eerily relevant, "mechanized petrification."

Leaders of Presbyterian Church USA once shared with me that they had been approached by leaders of a new denomination that was in its infancy, and were asked for counsel as to how they could develop structures like those of the PC(USA). The leaders of PC(USA) chuckled as they told me this story, saying "You don't want to become like us." For they knew that they were already trapped in a rational structure that had become irrational.

As Weber noted, the only answer for those trapped in an iron cage of modernity is to pay attention to what he called "charismatic prophets" and to recover "old ideals." In this moment of upheaval, disruption, and chaos, the wrong way for the dismantled Church to turn is back to the managers and the "new" ideals of modernity that got us trapped in the first place.

Folks, the Holy Spirit has broken the bars of that trap in this pandemic, and I for one am not going back into it. I hope you will join me as we wait upon God's Spirit to show us the road signs and guideposts that will lead us to that new heaven and new earth. It is the prophets and apostles who know the way home.

CHAPTER 37

"Conrad, Are You Suggesting We Shut Down Our Congregation?"
May 2021

A member of our congregation, with great sincerity, but clearly troubled, asked me this question: "Conrad, are you suggesting that we shut down our congregation?" The answer for me is clearly "No." As I write day after day, I think often of our grandson Ezra and how much I want for him to grow up in a community of faithful followers of Jesus and how thankful I am that his parents have chosen to be part of such a community.

My calling, as I sense it, is more descriptive of what is occurring in the Church than prescriptive of what should be for any particular church. I trust the providence of the Almighty to bring to pass in his time the eschatological future that has already been prescribed in heaven.

What is so clear to me is that the Church in the West/North is doing a pretty good job of shutting down itself—if one doesn't believe that, then one's eyes have to be closed. Gallup recently reported that only 47 percent of Americans now belong to a church, mosque, or synagogue; this is down from 70 percent in just 1999. This figure had remained at about 70 percent for the preceding six decades.[44]

So something is happening to the Church in America. Despite twenty years of emphasis on missional church, despite forty years of

---

[44] https://news.gallup.com/poll/341963/church-membership-falls-below-majority-first-time.aspx.

Evangelical efforts to find an ally in the political right, despite being the nation with more Christian radio stations, television channels, and a host of other resources, Gallup also reports that thousands of congregations are closing yearly.

In the early twentieth century, sociologist Émile Durkheim was the first in my discipline to use quantitative data to study a social problem. The problem he chose was suicide, which is not unrelated to the choices the Church is making today as it implodes upon itself. Durkheim argued that an individual is more likely to make an effort to take their life if they are socially isolated from others and if they have lost their grounding in the norms of society—that is, if they no longer know the rules of how to live and are lost in the social landscape of their lives. But he was clear that he could not predict which individuals would ultimately choose to end their lives, only that those who did so lacked social integration and a sense of what is normative.

I would argue the Church is in a similar way self-annihilating and for similar reasons. Simply put, the choices we have made have resulted in our being lost within the spiritual landscape. Like Christian in Bunyan's *Pilgrim's Progress*, we have left the King's highway for what appear like shortcuts to security and protection found in political leaders and party and in the process have lost sight of what is really true, good, right, and just.

The norms of the King's highway are simple: "Seek justice, love mercy, and walk humbly with your God." And yet these values and their expression in the Church seem like a distant echo. On this anniversary of the death of George Floyd, white Evangelicals are more concerned about what they perceive as the unrighteousness of the Black Lives Matter than about that part of the movement that is simply an extension of a biblically grounded Civil Rights movement and an example of what civil rights leader John Lewis called "good trouble." Evangelicals would prefer to bar the discussion of "critical race theory" than to recognize that our efforts to censor this discussion is grounded more in our desire to remain the oppressor than to join the oppressed in creating structural changes that would level the playing field and create the possibility of the church community described in Acts 2 and 4, where the believers had all things in common and sold their goods so that the poor might be cared for.

For years I have wondered if the U.S. Church was on the same track as the Church in Europe. But after observing the response of the Church to racial injustice, the election of 2020, the infighting about masking and non-masking, the embrace of theories ungrounded in data, and now these most recent data on the accelerating abandonment of the Church across all age groups, but especially among emerging adults, I no longer wonder.

Just as my body is being dismantled by Parkinson's disease and a force beyond my control these days, so the body of Christ that I love is being dismantled by our own efforts and choices. But as I've been noting for the last fifteen years—it is being dismantled by a Force and Spirit also beyond our control. For that Spirit is relentless and unhindered by our choices, and will bring that new heaven and new earth and that restored kingdom regardless of anything we do.

Which is why I am so moved by Dutch leader Henk Stenvers' words of surrender to the Holy Spirit and the dismantling of his own church. In the conclusion of his essay "Walking on Water," Stenvers says this:

> You can react to this in different ways. We can rest our weary heads on our hands and think, "This will never come out right," and give up. We can try to retain what we have and hold campaigns to increase membership. But we can also try to be open to a changed world and accept that things pass away and

new things turn up. In this way, we build on what was and is now, en route to what is new and as yet unfamiliar.

I am convinced that the last-named offers prospects for the future. Let us stop viewing the decline in membership as a problem that needs to be solved. Although our membership will no doubt decline even more substantially, those who are left—and it seems apparent, in other European countries, that 2,000 members is a kind of minimum—will be motivated, alert believers who will show great commitment to the community to which they belong.

I realize that this is asking a lot of us. As a faith community, we need to relinquish many things, many of which we greatly value. We need to have the faith to let go, even though we do not know what the future may bring. We need to trust that the faith community will find its purpose, to trust that we, building on tradition, will find ways to make the Mennonite voice heard, to witness of the imitation of Jesus in word and deed. We need to have faith in a future we do not yet know, resting in the Eternal One, who, as we proclaim again and again at Sunday services, does not abandon the works of his hands [Psalm 138:8 NIV]; we are nurtured by the stories about Jesus as they come to us in the Bible, and inspired by the Holy Spirit, who lifts us up beyond ourselves.

If we want to continue to exist, faith has to have priority. We are a community of God, our existence is legitimized by what drives us. In many cases, we need to stop "playing church" and, instead, return to the countermovement of the Mennonites. Perhaps we have gone too far in wanting to go along with the established churches in the past century and have forgotten what it was all about: following Jesus.

But to be able to do this, we need to reflect on why we actually want the story to continue. What is really our story for the world? What is our witness? Do we want to work for change, and let go, or do we prefer to keep everything as it always was? Do we have the courage to live with the uncertainty that goes with relinquishing security and walking unfamiliar paths, knowing that these, too, could be the wrong ones, to live in hope and anticipation, without, perhaps, seeing the final goal, living in the imitation of Christ?

The world is in chaos, and it is logical that we are afraid to be swallowed up in it. How, then, do you rise above the chaos? We are always talking about following Jesus. Do we believe in that story of Jesus, do we believe in Jesus, do we believe Jesus? Above all: do we believe what Jesus believed? Do we live up to it, or do we fear to do so? As in the story of Peter, do we look down and get startled by the water and start sinking? In that case, there is always the hand of Jesus reaching out to us; let us grasp it and face the unknown in faith, like people of the way. If you are en route, you can't cling to the old, or live in the security of the familiar view. En route, either walking or in the boat, there are always new views; every curve you take, every country you approach, gives a new vision of what can be.

Let us relinquish what is keeping us from heading out. It is better to be a community of people who choose for God and people en route, than a community of people who try to cling to what they have but consequently lose Jesus, God, the other, and ultimately themselves.

But this does not mean that we should relinquish everything with the idea that anything goes. Failing to put the imitation of Jesus in center place for fear of putting people off is no option. On the contrary, I am convinced that we are more attractive when we have a strong fundament—believing Jesus and believing what Jesus believed—than when we propagate a meaningless "everything goes." That is not a lack of freedom, but the basis for discussion.

To be a genuine faith community, and remain one, we

need to return to the content of our faith and place priority on the imitation of Jesus.[45]

Friends, see why this divinely inspired essay so moves me and gives me hope, and is really the answer I should have given to that church member who asked, "Are you suggesting we shut down the congregation?"

Thank you again, Henk, for hearing from the Spirit.

---

[45] Henk Stenvers, "Walking on Water," Part 1, "Concerning the Future of the Dutch Mennonites" (Algemene Doopsgezinde Societëit), Feb. 3, 2021, https://achurchdismantled.com/henk-stenvers-essay/.

CHAPTER 38

The Light at the End of the Tunnel
April 2021

In 2017, as part of a much needed sabbatical, Heidi and I traveled west, spending time at a retreat in Colorado Springs and then heading to the lovely Oregon coast. On our way, we stopped and rode the incredibly scenic Hiawatha Rails to Trail bike ride that begins high in the mountains of Montana and winds its way slowly downward across old trestle bridges and high above the valleys of Idaho below. It was the loveliest ride we have ever taken.

But that trail also includes a lengthy tunnel—about two miles in length. We debated going around it but decided to go through it. If the little kids over there could do it, what was wrong with us? We had been given a small and (as we would soon learn) somewhat useless flashlight to guide us through.

The challenge of tunnels like the one we rode through that day is that one so often sees the promise of light long before you ever get through the tunnel. That light does give much needed encouragement that the end of the darkness is ahead, but it does not give light to the current darkness. It offers hope, but that hope does itself not offer light.

In that tunnel on this day, we still had to negotiate water dripping from the ceiling, gigantic potholes, and mudpuddles that threatened to upend us at any moment and send us flying into the ground. We had to make our way around slower riders. We had to watch out for folks coming from the opposite direction who were also negotiating all of the things we were as well. We found ourselves keeping count of the mile markers along the path that told us how far until we were out of the darkness. Because that glimmer of light could not tell us where we were or how far we had to go—only that we were heading in the direction of the light.

Life is so like this sometimes. I am finding exiting from ministry to be like this. Exiting from a role is a fascinating and rich time of learning, and potentially one of personal growth. It offers the promise of light, and yet the very act of exiting also begins to reveal darkness, both in oneself and in one's social role and social context. How does one negotiate this darkness, found both in oneself and in the space one is leaving? The potholes and mudpuddles haven't miraculously disappeared. The other riders have not gone anywhere. The risks remain. What one is left with is the promise of the coming light—a light that heals, that comforts, that guides, and that surely beats the crummy flashlights we are holding onto for dear life right now.

But what one also realizes is that in this life, we will always remain somewhat tunneled—somewhat in the dark and the shadows—and that the light ahead will not be fully revealed nor will we step into it entirely until that last glorious morning when all is light and all is day—the fullest light and the grandest day!

This week I was reading Hebrews 2, where the author seems to understand and speak to the discomfort of seeing the Light while still in the dark: "But we do see Jesus," the writer echoes. In a place where we will for now always see through a glass darkly, some day we shall see "face to face," says Saint Paul, someone who more than anyone knew the reality of living in darkness and looking ahead to the light.

And that is our hope: that if we keep negotiating the potholes and mudpuddles and navigating our way around the other riders and counting the mile markers, and most of all keeping our eyes fixed on Jesus, then we will finally leave this darkness and enter into that Light, once and for all time, that we glimpse ahead and that keeps coaxing us: "You can do it. I know you can!"

Ω